T0154724

Robert O'Byrne is always impeccably dressed and groomed. He is one of Ireland's best-known writers on architecture, fine art, and design. Among his previous books are *Luggala*, *Romantic Irish Homes*, *Romantic English Homes* (all published by CICO Books), and *Living in Dublin*. Robert is based in County Meath, Ireland.

THE DRESS CODE

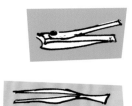

THE DRESS CODE

A MAN'S GUIDE TO FLAWLESS STYLE

ROBERT O'BYRNE

DOG 'n' BONE

This edition published in 2018 by Dog 'n' Bone Books
An imprint of Ryland Peters & Small Ltd

20–21 Jockey's Fields   341 E 116th St
London WC1R 4BW   New York, NY 10029

www.rylandpeters.com

10 9 8 7 6 5 4 3 2 1

First published as *The Perfectly Dressed Gentleman* in 2011 and
The Perfectly Groomed Gentleman in 2013 by CICO Books

Text © Robert O'Byrne 2011, 2013, 2018
Design and illustration © CICO Books 2018

A CIP catalog record for this book is available from the Library of
Congress and the British Library.

ISBN: 978 1 911026 66 2

Printed in China

Editor: Pete Jorgensen
Designer: Jerry Goldie
Design concept: Paul Tilby
Illustrator: Lord Dunsby aka Steve Millington

Contents

INTRODUCTION 6

Introduction

**As many definitions of what constitutes a
gentleman exist as naysayers prepared to decry
the decline in gentlemanly standards. "A true
gentleman," said Oscar Wilde, "is one who is never
unintentionally rude," while the 18th-century
English physician Dr Thomas Fuller pronounced
that a gentleman "is a man who can disagree
without being disagreeable." However, universal
agreement will never be reached on what
attributes are necessary for someone to be
esteemed a gentleman, not least because the term
itself has long been in a state of evolution.**

The word gentle derives from the Latin adjective *gentilis* meaning "of
or belonging to the same family, group, or race." The notion of
a gentleman emerged during the Middle Ages when such men,
while not necessarily noble, were individuals entitled and
expected to bear arms in defense of their monarch and country. In
other words, they were members of a warrior caste.

This narrow definition of gentlemanliness began to broaden
in the Renaissance with the emergence of princely courts at which
the well-bred and wealthy were required to be in attendance. In
order to flourish in the competitive courtly environment, men had
to learn how to behave in company, a process assisted by the
publication of guides to civility such as Baldassare Castiglione's

Il Libro del Cortegiano (The Book of the Courtier), which appeared in 1528. This stressed not only the importance of skill at arms but also the advantages of good manners, and how to be polite and considerate. Instruction from informed sources was of importance, but so too was moving in well-bred society: An English proverb has it that "Education begins a gentleman, conversation completes him."

Castiglione's book had enormous influence throughout Europe during the following centuries and helped to formulate the modern definition of a gentleman, one that gradually became dependent not so much on birth as behavior. This interpretation of gentlemanliness fully emerged in the 19th century with the rise of a bourgeoisie whose male members enjoyed the advantages of money but not high social rank. They wished to be regarded as gentlemen and so sought to emphasize the value of education and good manners.

While of primary significance today, this aspect of the gentleman's character has probably always been present to some extent. As the priest John Ball rhetorically asked during the Peasants' Revolt of 1381, "When Adam delved and Eve span, who then was the gentleman?" And in the 17th century a woman supposedly once asked James II to make her son a gentleman, to which the king responded, "I could make him a nobleman, but God Almighty could not make him a gentleman." In other words, regardless of origins anyone can be judged a gentleman provided he conforms to certain behavioral strictures, such as displaying consideration for other people. Different cultures will have their own rules of etiquette but a concern for the needs of society at large and an interest in the welfare of those he encounters are the hallmarks of the modern gentleman.

What does any of this have to do with grooming and how we men dress ourselves? More than you might appreciate. Once we move out of our private space and into the public arena, we should give thought to our appearance and whether it might cause disquiet or even offense. It could be, and often is, argued that how each of us dresses and presents ourselves ought to be a matter of personal concern and irrelevant to anyone else. Whether it is piercings and tattoos or low-slung jeans that expose underwear, claims of personal expression are justified with the same defense: It's my business how I dress. In theory a case can be made on such grounds, but it presumes our own opinions and interests are more important than those of the rest of society. Because a gentleman would never agree with such an assertion, it follows that in matters of dress, hygiene, as in every other aspect of his life, he will always give consideration to the interests of the world in which he moves, however irrational they might seem. If, for example, he receives a wedding invitation stipulating a formal dress code, this is what he will wear. To do otherwise would be to put his own inclinations ahead of his hosts' and that would be ungentlemanly. What some might castigate as conformism, a gentleman regards as consideration.

A gentleman takes both personal and public interest into account and dresses accordingly. That way he pleases not only himself but whoever meets him.

PART ONE

Perfect Dress Sense

CHAPTER 1

The Suit

Contrary to popular opinion, a good suit can serve an infinite variety of roles and be adapted to almost any circumstance. Just as many women rely on an LBD (Little Black Dress) to see them through many different occasions, so a gentleman will find a Good Dark Suit—which should perhaps henceforth be known as the GDS—invaluable.

The Origins of the Suit

In the pages ahead, it will be stated more than once that men's clothing as it exists today originated in England at the start of the 19th century and is particularly indebted to one man: George "Beau" Brummell. But the suit's starting point goes back further, to the 17th century and the restoration of Charles II to the English throne. Prior to this period, the suit did not exist; while men may have worn short jackets, they were teamed with doublet and hose.

In February 1661 diarist Samuel Pepys noted that he had worn his "coate," which was "the manner now among gentlemen." The coate in question was of a length similar to the modern overcoat and was a somewhat fitted variation on a garment worn by men when riding. Five years later, in October 1666 Pepys recorded that the king "begins to put on his vest," this being what Americans still know as a vest but the British call a waistcoat. Thus the three-piece suit began to appear, especially when English countrymen who, unlike their French counterparts, did not care to attend court had such sets of clothing made in the same plain wool cloth to wear at home on their country estates.

Anglomania in respect of clothing has a long history and one of its key dates is the publication in 1774 of the German writer Johann Wolfgang von Goethe's *The Sorrows of Young Werther*. The hero of this proto-romantic novel dresses in the English style—that is to say in a plain tailcoat, vest/waistcoat, trousers, and boots—and Goethe's book inspired a mania among sensitive young men to dress likewise. One of the features of the French Revolution was the emergence of the Sans-culottes—the men whose break with the Ancien Régime was symbolized by their abandonment of court knee breeches in preference for English-style suiting.

In the opening years of the 19th century, the most significant contribution made by Beau Brummell was to work with tailors in London. Together they focused on creating clothes that fitted the body and followed its line precisely; prior to Brummell's appearance this had not been deemed a matter of importance. Brummell was a plain dresser, unconcerned with rich fabrics or elaborate finishes. Instead he concentrated on perfection of silhouette, achieved through careful cut of fabric and exact tailoring. His rise in influence coincided with an increasing sophistication among London's tailors,

Brummell paid particular attention to the perfection of silhouette, achieved through careful cut of fabric and exact tailoring

> *You will find a good suit enhances your wardrobe and its absence will leave you sartorially poorer*

many of whom, then as now, were based in Savile Row, Mayfair. The simple but supremely elegant style of dress advocated by both Brummell and his tailors was soon universally adopted, hence the emergence of the Good Dark Suit that remains an indispensable feature of the male wardrobe.

The Suit Today

Although once almost revolutionary in its connotations, for the past half-century the suit has come to be associated with conservatism and is shunned by any aspiring radical. On the other hand, all men who wish to be considered respectable and conforming members of society will don a suit. For similar reasons, some men own what they designate their "interview suit," a somber item worn whenever they wish to make a good impression. Suits are also associated with formal occasions, not just a job interview but also weddings, funerals, and so forth. They can be judged stuffy and uncomfortable, although anyone who finds them so is clearly not wearing a well-designed piece of clothing because a good suit should be as imperceptible to the wearer as a second skin.

In the 1990s some businesses that had hitherto expected their employees to wear a suit abandoned this prerequisite, and many newer companies, especially those in the technology sector, began almost to frown on suits as somehow inhibiting creativity. Nevertheless, certain professions like banking and law, as well as senior management in most fields, still expect their practitioners to wear a suit, as do large sections of the service industry. Thus the derogatory term "suits" describes men who are believed to have sacrificed their individuality to corporate conventionality. This is a mistaken view: You will find the possession of a good suit enhances your wardrobe and its absence will leave you sartorially poorer than should be the case. No man who aspires to be well dressed can do without a suit.

Bespoke

The term bespoke, which means custom-made, derives from having a cloth or garment "spoken for." In other words, it is the male equivalent of women's couture: something made specifically to your measurements by an accredited tailor. Ideally you should own at least one bespoke suit. It goes without saying that acquiring such an item is going to be an expensive enterprise but this will prove a worthwhile investment.

Whereas most women are familiar with their body size and shape, the same is not true of the average male. Next time you're in a public place, look at the men around you and notice how if they are wearing a jacket, almost without exception this is the wrong size; most commonly it will be too big for the frame beneath. A tailor will provide you with correct measurements, those specific to your body (most men's shoulders, for example, slope more on one side than the other), a piece of information that will be invaluable when you

A bespoke suit is as good as a gym membership—both make sure you take care of yourself

subsequently buy ready-to-wear clothing. In addition, the high cost of purchasing a bespoke suit ensures that you take care of both the garment and your body—there's no point in spending all that money and then six months later discovering that you've put on weight and can no longer fit into the pants or button the jacket. In this respect, a bespoke suit is as good as a gym membership—both make sure you take care of yourself.

Creating the Perfect Fit

The process of having a bespoke suit made for you is as follows. You begin by consulting your chosen tailor over such matters as cut, cloth, and style of the garment before careful measurements of your body are taken. A pattern is then made specific to you, and this will be used to chalk out and cut the selected fabric. After lining, canvases, pockets, buttons, and so forth have been also prepared, the individual parts are sewn together in anticipation of a first fitting on the client. This is called the baste stage, after which a new pattern may have to be created, the suit stitching ripped out, the cloth recut, and other necessary adjustments made. Additional structural work is now performed before a second fitting. At this stage, the suit ought to fit the client without fault, but, should it be required, further alterations will be made before collar and sleeves are sewn in, buttonholes and edge stitching completed by hand, and so on. Then, after a final press, the finished garment is ready for a last fitting and presentation.

It will be appreciated that length of time and attention to detail account for the cost of a bespoke suit. As a less expensive alternative, there is made-to-measure in which many of the same processes are followed, but rather than a new pattern being made, an existing one that most closely corresponds to the client's measurements is used, albeit with individual adjustments. In addition, whereas bespoke involves hand-sewing, made-to-measure uses machine stitching, although some details may be finished by hand. Obviously price is a factor here, with made-to-measure being notably cheaper but still providing a better fit than does ready-to-wear, which depends on average sizing and fails to take the particular customer's body shape into account.

The Business Suit

The most common suit style worn today is the business suit, also known as the lounge suit in Britain. As already mentioned, the suit evolved from clothing worn by country gentlemen and, despite its name, this is also true of the business suit. There are enormous variations within the basic theme, depending on whether the suit in question closes with one, two, or three buttons, is single- or double-breasted, has a single or double vent at the back, and so forth. Then there are decisions to be made about the cloth, cut, color, and pattern.

When these factors are taken into account, it becomes evident that the reason for the suit's enduring success is its versatility: No two need ever be the same. It is no wonder that in recent decades so many women, appreciating its innumerable merits, have also adopted the suit as their preferred mode of dress.

If price is a factor, made-to-measure is cheaper than bespoke but provides a better fit than ready-to-wear

The Jacket

The key element in the suit is the jacket, since this determines the overall silhouette. It is also the part of any suit over which most trouble will have been taken in production.

Button Placement

Jackets are either single- or double-breasted. Shorter and heavier-built men are advised to keep away from the double-breasted style since it will only draw attention to their physique. Only half the outside buttons on a double-breasted jacket function because the second row is solely for show. There are typically four or six buttons in total, with the upper pair being half again as far apart as each of the lower pairs. A double-breasted jacket can look extremely stylish provided it is well tapered from shoulder to waist. Otherwise, as was the fashion in the 1980s, it will seem excessively boxy.

The male jacket buttons left side over right, supposedly because in the days when swords were carried a right-handed man could reach for the hilt of his weapon with ease. If you are portly, wear a single-breasted jacket with lower placed buttons as this will increase the vertical line and make you look leaner. Jackets usually have either two or three buttons but you will also find examples with a single-button fastening; these are usually darted to give a narrow outline and therefore look best on slim men. If closing the front of your

Always leave the bottom button of your jacket unfastened, not least because this will make it easier for you to put a hand in your pants pocket

jacket, only use the upper button (with a two-button fastening) or the middle one (with three). If you insist on buttoning through your jacket, it will have the effect of making you appear constrained. Always leave the bottom button unfastened, not least because this will make it easier for you to put a hand into your pants pocket. Likewise, when you sit down unbutton your jacket, otherwise it will strain against your body (and you also risk creasing it across the back). Your jacket ought to fasten comfortably over the chest and not gape open when buttoned; if it does so, then you're wearing too large a size.

The Correct Fit

In addition a jacket should fit tidily across the back and not hang off the shoulders; the last of these is a common failing precisely because men are unfamiliar with their correct size. Because of the English tradition in tailoring, English suits tend to have defined but not exaggerated shoulder lines, a tapered side, and two vents at the back, all contributing to a Y-shaped silhouette. Italian suits, which became fashionable in the 1980s, have a stronger, wider shoulder line—even when, as introduced by Giorgio Armani, they have no padding—and hang looser on the torso without vents at the back. American suits occupy a ground somewhere between these two, with a certain amount of both shoulder definition and tapering.

Lapel Styles

The jacket lapel derives from 18th-century coats which buttoned up to the neck. When the top of the coat was left open, the ends of the closure fell back to expose the lining, and during the following century this feature of the jacket was gradually formalized into the creased lapels we know, fronted in the same fabric as the rest of the garment with the lining no longer visible.

There are different styles of lapels: the notched or stepped which only befits single-breasted suits, the peaked (much seen on double-breasted suits and dinner jackets), the shawl, and others such as Mandarin collars. On a single-breasted, sharply tapered suit a peaked lapel can look extremely smart. The left lapel should have a buttonhole intended to hold a boutonniere, which is a decorative flower.

The Purpose of Pockets

Jackets tend to have a variety of interior and exterior pockets. Those inside the jacket are intended to hold items such as wallets and in recent years cell phones, but it is advisable not to put too much into them as it distorts the garment's shape. On the outside, there will be one upper breast pocket on the left-hand side; this can hold a pocket handkerchief either decorative or functional in intent. Below will be two pockets, one each at left and right. The patch pocket is a single piece of cloth stitched onto the jacket; essentially casual in style, it suits sports and linen jackets but does not become formal suiting. The flap pocket is seen on most business suits, the pocket being contained inside the main body of the jacket and marked by a lined flap of fabric. These pockets run in a horizontal line except in instances where the pocket is slanted (called a hacking pocket because it was first created to allow a hand to slip easily into the pocket while out riding). On the right-hand side of the jacket you sometimes find another, smaller pocket above the main flap pocket; this is known as a ticket pocket, its original purpose being to hold a train ticket.

The ideal jacket cuff length should allow about half an inch of the shirt beneath to be seen

Finally, formalwear such as the dinner jacket usually has two jetted pockets, enclosed within the garment with the slit marked by a small strip of fabric along the top. Jackets usually come with their pockets stitched shut; it is advisable to leave them this way to stop you using the pockets to carry items and ruining the line of your garment.

Sleeve Length

Jacket sleeves should not be baggy but nor ought they to be cut so tight that it becomes impossible to lift your arms over your head with ease. Jacket sleeves end in a row of buttons which traditionally could be undone; where this is still possible the style has the self-explanatory name of "surgeon's cuff." Rarely found in ready-to-wear, these remain a distinguishing feature of bespoke suits. Otherwise cuff buttons are purely decorative and number anywhere between one and four, the latter being most common today on business suit jackets. The ideal jacket cuff length should allow about half an inch (1cm) of the shirt beneath to be seen. A century ago, some jacket sleeves had turn-back cuffs two inches (5cm) deep and these are still occasionally seen.

One Vent or Two?

The vent on the tail of your jacket once served the purpose of allowing the wearer to ride a horse without sitting on his coat. While this may no longer be the case, they still help to ensure the hang of a jacket is preserved, especially while sitting down. Italian-designed and some casual jackets tend to have no vent, but the alternatives are a single or double vent, the second of these being typical of English tailoring. As a rule, dinner jackets do not have vents.

Fabric

One of the great, but rarely acknowledged, changes in clothing to have occurred over the past century is the weight of our clothes; today, thanks to better heating at home and in the workplace, we dress more lightly than did our forebears. As a consequence of central heating all sorts of new fabric blends have been created, especially by Italian mills, to offer the consumer more flexibility and ease of dressing.

Nevertheless, when it comes to suiting, nothing is better than medium-weight worsted pure wool, preferably taken from merino sheep. Despite recent competition from new fibers, wool remains the best choice for a gentleman's suit because it is natural, breathes well, provides good insulation, and is exceptionally durable (thanks to their natural elasticity, wool fibers resist tearing and can bend back on themselves more than 20,000 times without breaking, unlike cotton which breaks after 3,200 bends). Made from wool, worsted yarns are hard-wearing and yet light, and therefore much used for suiting. During the course of the last century, they were produced in ever-finer weights and are now the cloth of choice for city suits.

Wool Variants

Tweed is a woolen fabric with an altogether rougher finish, suitable for countrywear being moisture-resistant and hard-wearing. The two most famous tweeds are Harris from Scotland and Donegal from

Ireland, but lighter, finer tweeds, some of them incorporating varying quantities of silk, are also produced elsewhere. Tweed remains an essentially rural cloth and as a rule is not seen in an urban setting, except when used for a weekend jacket.

Invented in 1879 by Thomas Burberry (founder of the still extant clothing company), gabardine is another tough, tightly woven woolen cloth appropriate for suiting and identifiable by its diagonal ribbed surface.

Mohair is a silk-like cloth with a characteristic high sheen that comes from the Angora goat. Warm, water-resistant, and durable, it is considered a luxury fiber, as is cashmere which likewise comes from goats and is particularly fine and smooth to the touch.

Flannel is a soft woven fabric made from carded wool. It used to be popular for business suiting—in the mid-1950s author Sloan Wilson wrote a best-selling novel called *The Man in the Gray Flannel Suit*—but has since fallen out of favor and now tends to be more often used for casual jackets.

Alternative Fabrics

Jackets and suits are sometimes made of velvet and its near relation corduroy, with the former fabric most often employed in the production of evening wear. The best, and most expensive, velvet is made of silk, with a less costly version produced in cotton. In recent years technological advances have led to the creation of a variety of entirely synthetic velvets, or velvets produced from a mix of natural and man-made fibers. The tufted pile of velvet gives it a uniquely tactile quality, enhanced by the cloth's reflective sheen, hence the appeal for evening wear.

Corduroy is in effect a ridged variant of velvet, with alternating tufts and patches of bare base fabric. Corduroy can have different widths, the size of which is known as the "wale," this being the number of ridges per inch (2.5cm), so the lower the wale, the thicker the raised tufts. Standard wale of 11 per inch is used for pants, while jackets are most often made of pincord or needlecord corduroy with a wale of 16 or more per inch.

A number of lighter-weight cloths are used for summer suiting and, while these will not necessarily find a place in the office environment, they are ideal for occasions when semiformal dressing is required. Among the most notable fabrics is cotton, in particular when manufactured as seersucker. First used for suits in colonial India, seersucker is so woven that some threads bunch together to give the finished cloth an uneven surface, which in turn means it sits slightly away from the surface of the skin and is cool to wear. Seersucker often comes in stripes of white and another color, commonly blue or gray.

Linen has long been used for summer suiting. The textile is made from fibers of the flax plant and is renowned for its absorbent qualities and coolness. With a natural luster, it can be dyed almost any color, but for suit jackets and pants is commonly white or ivory. Linen absorbs and loses moisture with ease, but it soon becomes wrinkled and for some men this is a drawback because their appearance can thus look crumpled. On the other hand, that slightly battered quality is part of its charm and linen grows softer with age and washing, making it also popular for casual shirts. Whether you take to it rather depends on how sharply turned out you wish to be on all occasions.

Color and Pattern

If you're going to own only one top-notch suit, best make it in a single color and one that offers maximum versatility. Black is funereal and oppressive (and, you'll soon discover, shows every speck of dirt). Blue is an option but finding the right shade of navy—not too dark but not too bright either—can take up a lot of time. Frankly, brown for city suits is simply not to be countenanced; it is essentially a country color and looks out of place in the urban environment. Charcoal gray, on the other hand, complements every skin tone, works with every color and pattern of shirt, and successfully manages the dressed-up/dressed-down formula. A good medium-weight gray suit is at home in the business environment, plus the jacket can be worn without the pants and instead teamed with jeans or chinos. So, a charcoal gray suit should be the centerpiece of your classic wardrobe. Of course you really should have more than a single suit, particularly if you are obliged to wear one every day. No garment can be worn on successive days without suffering; it should be left to rest in between. If you buy judiciously, wait for seasonal sales to make your purchases. Stick to classic styles and take trouble to look after your clothes and it should be possible very quickly to build up a collection of good suits that will last you for many years to come.

Charcoal gray complements all skin tones, works with every color and pattern of shirt, and capably manages the dressed-up or dressed-down formula

Pinstripe has become associated with two very different sectors of society: banking and the Mafia

Acceptable Patterns

With a few extreme exceptions, suit patterns are limited to herringbone, stripes, and checks, but do not be discouraged by this apparent restriction. Rather like suit styling, within a supposedly tight framework the imaginative dresser will discover the possibilities of almost infinite variety.

Herringbone is created by cloth being made in a broken-twill weave. This produces threads running alternately from left to right and forming an inverted V-effect not unlike the bones of a herring. Usually in wool, it is very popular for suiting.

Stripes traditionally take two forms: the chalk and the pin, with the first being visibly wider than the second. They can be found on cloth of all colors, usually black, blue, and gray. The vertical stripe is especially advantageous for shorter or stockier men, since it gives the impression of lengthening their silhouette. Pinstripe has become associated with two very different sectors of society: banking and the Mafia, both of which want to convey respectability, albeit for dissimilar reasons. Although it can sometimes look stuffy, when seen on a well-cut suit pinstripe or chalk-stripe is immensely stylish.

More variation is found in suit checks, among the more popular being houndstooth, a duotone pattern achieved by intertwining dark and light threads to produce a small checkered effect supposedly resembling the teeth of a dog. The other common check is glen plaid, a woven twill design intermingling small and large checks, usually in black and white but perhaps incorporating a third color. Glen plaid is also known as Prince of Wales check, since it was often worn by the Duke of Windsor while he held the former title. Glen plaid can be smart but, as with so much else, should be worn with care by the heavily built. Incidentally, tartan must be avoided by anyone who is not Scottish or a punk.

Other Styles of Jackets

In addition to suits, your wardrobe should hold a number of other jackets which will come into their own on semiformal and casual occasions. Here are the main categories.

The tweed jacket is a hardy perennial, not least thanks to the varieties of weights, colors, and patterns in which tweed is available. Such jackets started to be worn in the middle of the 19th century, initially by ghillies (fishing/hunting guides) and gamekeepers on Scottish estates but their practical appeal meant similar items were soon being produced for the owners of these estates and their friends, and demand quickly spread ever wider until today when the tweed jacket enjoys universal appeal. With its lightly defined shoulder line, single or double vent, and front flap pockets, you will find ownership of one or more tweed jackets invaluable, since they are highly adaptable, working well with any style of pants, shirt, or knitwear, capable of being smartened up or toned down according to what is worn with them. Choose tweed of medium weight as you do not want to become overly hot while wearing the jacket.

The hacking jacket is most often made of tweed but has a couple of particular characteristics, not least the diagonally slanting pockets which indicate the jacket's origins as a style to be worn when on horseback (the pocket being so shaped that they were easier for the rider to access in these circumstances). Hacking jackets as a rule have strongly defined shoulders, a darted body to define the waist, a high-buttoning front, and a single rear vent. They may be made of tweed or some other hard-wearing cloth, such as cavalry twill or gabardine.

The sports jacket is another variation on the same theme, often made in cashmere (or a wool/cashmere mix), flannel, or something similar. It will usually have patch pockets and be relaxed in styling with a loose cut to the body.

The blazer takes its name from the bright red cloth used to make the jackets first worn by the rowing club of St John's College, Cambridge in 1825; another legend has it that the term derives from the jackets worn by sailors on *HMS Blazer* but this is frequently called into question. In fact, the garment worn by the Cambridge rowers was closer to what would now be called a boating jacket than the blazer, which stylistically is a descendant of the reefer jacket, also known as the pea coat, a double-breasted garment worn by sailors when they were engaged in activities such as reefing a ship's sails. These jackets gradually evolved into the modern blazer and became single- as well as double-breasted, and made of lightweight wool. This variation is only one of many that can be found in blazers today, since they might have flap or patch pockets and horn or metal buttons (a memory of their naval origins), and be cut close to the body or have a more relaxed shape.

But whatever its attributes, every blazer will be navy in color and possess the same quality as a good tweed jacket: the ability to be called into service in almost every circumstance. You can wear a blazer with a shirt and tie or with an open-necked polo shirt. It can be accompanied with equal success by gray flannel pants, jeans, or even shorts. In other words, it is highly adaptable and for that reason you owe it to yourself to have one. Blazers, habitually with a badge on the breast pocket or some colored piping around lapels and cuffs, are worn to indicate membership of a club or sporting organization, or else attendance at a particular school or college.

The Waistcoat

The origins of the waistcoat, or the vest as it is also known, can be precisely dated. In October 1666, Samuel Pepys wrote in his diary that Charles II "hath yesterday in council declared his resolution of setting a fashion for clothes which he will never alter. It will be a vest, I know not well how." This garment, today known as a waistcoat, was inspired by the vests seen by English travelers to the Persian court of Shah Abbas who brought news of them back to England.

For a long time, men's "vests" were as elaborate and richly embroidered as the coats worn over them. It was only when male dress underwent a radical purification in the early 19th century that waistcoats became less elaborate, although a residue of that old style can still be seen in the fancy waistcoats worn by men participating in formal occasions such as weddings. In addition, whereas the 17th- and 18th-century vests had been long, the modern waistcoat as it emerged in the Regency era was shorter, stopping at the waist (hence the term waistcoat). Dandies like Beau Brummell recognized the waistcoat's potential to enhance the rest of a man's costume, and to act as a figure-molder by exaggerating the chest (sometimes with the assistance of concealed padding) and pulling in the waist. With whalebone stiffeners at the front and lacings to the rear, Victorian waistcoats acted as surrogate corsets for men. Although these features later disappeared, the waistcoat remained a part of men's clothing until the mid-20th century, especially when a suit was being worn and in part because it provided additional warmth in cold weather.

Improvements in heating and the growth in popularity of knitwear led to a decline in waistcoat wearing, but there have been periodic revivals in popularity, such as when they were worn by John Travolta in 1977's *Saturday Night Fever*. And they have remained an essential part of dress among senior figures in certain professions like banking and law. Of course, many young men today wear waistcoats without an accompanying jacket and even without shirts, replacing the latter with a T-shirt.

Wearing Your Waistcoat

A classic waistcoat is made of the same fabric as the suit jacket and pants, will have six buttons and four pockets: two at the breast, two closer to the waistband. An adjustable strap at the back will help to tighten the lower section of the garment, the back being made either of the same material as the front or else of satin. It is traditional to leave the bottom button of the waistcoat unfastened, supposedly because this is what Edward VII did when his stomach had expanded in middle age. The waistcoat should end just below the waistband of your pants, so that no sign of the belt can be seen; a gap between the two is unsightly. Similarly, when the front of your jacket is fastened, only the topmost button of the waistcoat should be visible.

Whether a waistcoat has lapels or not is a matter of personal taste, but bear in mind that it will add extra fabric and therefore may bulk out the silhouette. Your waistcoat must sit flush with your chest and not bulge out, so it is important that the fit be correct. Tailors will confirm that this is a technically difficult garment to produce and it is easy for it to destroy rather than improve your overall appearance.

Suit Pants

Whether a waistcoat is present or not, no suit can be given such a name unless it features a matching jacket and pants. The second of these garments is usually given less attention than jackets are. But pants have to suffer the greater wear and tear, so if possible, buy two pairs when purchasing a new suit (especially if it is bespoke). Your pants should fit well around the waist and not need to be held up by a belt, even though you will, of course, wear one of these or else a pair of suspenders, known as braces in Britain. Pants that are too loose will leave puckered fabric around the waist and ruin the chances of producing a smooth line. Likewise the legs of your pants should be neither too tight nor too baggy, allowing easy movement when required.

Creases, Cuffs, and Pleats

The crease down the front of each leg is a relative innovation, dating only from the end of the 19th century, around the same time that cuffs, or turn-ups, at the bottom of pants also made their debut. Today a sharp-centered crease in your pants will always look smart, just as its absence will suggest scruffiness. The only pants in which center creases are not deemed acceptable are jeans; there is no logic in this opinion but it is widespread.

Cuffs are conventionally regarded as unsuitable for business suits and formal wear, but fine for more casual dressing. They ought to be between an inch and an inch and a half (2.5–4cm) in depth. Shorter men are advised not to adopt cuffs as they can have the effect of making a pant leg look shorter than is the case. With or without a cuff, pant legs ought to be long enough to "break" on the front of the shoe and then have a small single fold before they begin their rise.

Pleats at the front of pants were commonly seen in the 1980s and '90s but in recent years have been less popular. There may be anything between one and four pleats on pants; those opening toward the side pockets are called reverse pleats while those opening toward the center are called forward pleats. Flat-fronted pants convey a smoother overall look to a suit and also increase the impression of leg length. For a long time pant flies were fastened by buttons, a feature still found both on clothes produced by traditional companies and, by contrast, on jeans. On the other hand, zippers are easier to fasten and give the front of pants a flatter line.

CHAPTER 2

The Coat

Overcoats are extremely practical items of clothing and you ought to have several in your wardrobe, distinguished from one another by color and material which will, in turn, mark them out for different occasions. Today the primary function of an overcoat remains what it has always been: to exclude cold and dirt.

———◆———

Before the advent of central heating, the possession of a thick coat was more necessary than is now the case. Nevertheless, since all of us have to venture outdoors—even if only occasionally—they retain their purpose, especially as global warming seems to have made our winters colder than ever before.

Moreover, as is often remarked today, when a man sheds or dons his coat he also makes a statement, thereby either announcing his arrival or declaring his imminent departure. Likewise, retaining your coat while indoors announces more clearly than could any words an intention not to linger. Thus coats possess their own language, one further emphasized by variations in fabric weight, design, and shade.

A Coat to Suit the Occasion

Ideally you ought to own a decent winter coat of substance, one that will provide ample protection from the elements in cold weather. A second coat of lighter weight and intended for town wear is also advantageous. In addition you will want to possess a raincoat and perhaps a coat for evenings and formal occasions.

The last of these will be black, but the color of your other coats should depend on personal taste and the circumstances in which they are most often to be worn. If you live in the country, for example, a tweed coat in mixed colors might be suitable, while for city dwellers something in a wool/cashmere mix and a shade of dark blue or gray would be the best option. Other factors will determine length, longer coats hanging more kindly on the frames of tall, slim men than on those of their shorter, stouter counterparts. Likewise, double-breasted coats—which used to be the norm until the late Victorian era—rarely look well on men carrying extra weight, since they draw attention to this disposition; if you have a heavy build, opt for a single-breasted coat and never one with a belt, or it could focus the eye on your midriff.

Finally, an overcoat, when teamed with gloves, scarf, and perhaps a hat, "finishes" an ensemble and indicates to observers what it means to be properly dressed. Especially on formal occasions, a man without a coat will always look wanting.

Like so much of men's dress, the overcoat as we know it today is a descendant of early 19th-century fashion. As is often the case, coats owe at least some of their present characteristics to military dress—the length of the coat and its vent at the back cut high meaning this garment could be worn while riding a horse, and still keep the wearer well covered and warm.

Choosing a Style

Some styles of coats are little seen today, such as the Ulster, which was made of a hard-wearing fabric like tweed and came with a shoulder cape over the sleeves; this feature disappeared around the beginning of the 20th century and the Ulster has been in decline ever since. So too the Inverness, a formal coat with long winged open sleeves that used to be worn with evening dress.

On the other hand, the Chesterfield, which originated in the 19th century, is the ancestor of most of today's overcoats. It is long, to the knees or even a little below, with no horizontal seam around the waist or sidebodies and a plain back, but the body can be somewhat shaped by judicious use of side seams and darts. A staple of the modern man's wardrobe, the Chesterfield can be either single- or double-breasted and be made in various weights of wool, cashmere, or a mix of both. As a formal coat, its palette is limited to black, gray, and navy. The best-known manufacturer of the Chesterfield-style coat is Crombie, a Scottish company in business since 1805, the name of which has become generic for coats of this type.

A variation on this theme is the covert coat, made in beige- or fawn-colored twill. Originally intended for the country, its relatively light weight means this item is now more often worn as a city coat with a suit beneath. The classic covert has a fly front closure, two side pockets (and a smaller ticket pocket), a velvet collar, and four lines of stitching at the cuffs and around the bottom hem.

The Chesterfield is the ancestor of most of today's coats and is a staple of the modern man's wardrobe

The polo coat is an American variant of the Chesterfield, believed to date from a century ago when polo players sought something to throw over their shoulders for warmth between chukkers. It is immediately identifiable by being made from plush, honey-toned camel hair and double-breasted. Other features can include thick sleeve cuffs, patch pockets, a half- or full belt, and white mother-of-pearl buttons. There is something inherently luxurious about a polo coat and it has long been favored by the exceptionally wealthy, not least because it is a visibly expensive purchase.

The Raglan is not too dissimilar from the Chesterfield except that it lacks shoulder seams so that each sleeve's upper side runs straight to the neckline, with a diagonal seam from underarm to collarbone. Its name comes from the 1st Baron Raglan, who lost his right arm following injuries that he sustained in 1815 at the Battle of Waterloo. The Raglan coat is customarily buttoned through, with a loose body and no belt.

The Loden coat is identifiable by its color, a deep green, and by its cloth, first woven by peasants living in the Austrian region of Loderers in the 16th century. The fabric is made from coarse oily wool of mountain sheep, which undergoes a process of shrinking so that it has the dense texture of felt before the nap is brushed and clipped, the result being a lightweight but tough cloth. Designed to be worn by huntsmen, the traditional Loden coat is unlined and has a deep center vent down the back (to allow freedom of movement), a double layer of material on the shoulders, and a covered fly-front.

Today the Duffel coat is liable to be associated with geeks, members of the old British Labour Party, and Paddington Bear; it is rarely the choice for anyone fashion-conscious. The name derives from the town of Duffel in Belgium where this style is believed to have originated. Aside from the coarse, heavy wool and tartan lining

*Occasionally adopted by members
of indie bands, the Duffel looks likely
to remain a minority taste*

used in its production, the two other distinctive traits of the Duffel are its hood and its toggle fastenings. The coat is not darted, falling straight to just above the knee. Occasionally adopted by members of indie bands, the Duffel looks likely to remain a minority taste.

As already observed, in addition to these coats, you will want to own at least one garment suitable for giving protection from rain. The classic of this genre is the Mackintosh, named after its Scottish originator Charles Macintosh who began selling his patented waterproof coats of rubberized fabric in the mid-1820s. Traditional Mackintoshes, otherwise known as "macs," continue to be produced and sold today, both their method of manufacture and their design having been updated in the intervening two centuries. Nevertheless, an authentic coat must be made of rubberized or rubber-laminated fabric.

The Mackintosh should be distinguished from the trench coat, which as its name indicates was originally created to be worn by soldiers fighting in the trenches during World War I. They needed an alternative to their heavy wool greatcoats and a trench coat fitted the bill.

Two British companies, Aquascutum and Burberry, both lay claim to have invented this garment, but the latter certainly patented the cloth from which it was made: gabardine. Water- and wind-resistant, gabardine is a tough, tightly woven worsted wool or cotton twill weave. In style, the trench coat still shows its military origins, with shoulder tabs and cuff straps, a storm flap by the collar, and a belt carrying several D-shaped rings, the last of these allowing soldiers to attach various items of equipment to their coat. Unlike Mackintoshes, trench coats are not waterproof. Nor do they provide ample warmth in very cold weather. But in the aftermath of World War I they became popular among civilians and started to make regular appearances in films, often worn by private detectives and by anti-heroes such as Humphrey Bogart's Rick Blaine in 1942's *Casablanca*. The trench coat has never since lost its romantic aura.

Finally, there is an item of clothing traditionally worn in the countryside but now as often seen in an urban setting: the Barbour. This is a coat made by J. Barbour & Sons Ltd, a British business established at the end of the 19th century and renowned for the hardy construction and durability of its waterproof waxed cotton fabric. Among aficionados, at least part of a Barbour's appeal is precisely its apparent indestructibility; the older and more battered the coat, the more it is cherished. Although the company has created new designs to take into account contemporary taste, the original Barbour cannot really be described as an object of great beauty. On the other hand, whatever the style it will keep the wearer warm and dry, and this helps to explain why city dwellers have adopted the Barbour in such large numbers.

CHAPTER 3

Shirts

The world's oldest preserved garment, dating back to around 3000 BCE. and made of linen, is a shirt discovered in Egypt by the archaeologist Flinders Petrie in 1912. This demonstrates that despite undergoing various permutations over the centuries, the shirt has been a staple of men's dressing for at least five millennia.

———◆———

Originally it was a tunic, often worn loose and made of linen; both characteristics demonstrated the wearer's wealth because only the affluent could afford the extravagance of such an ample garment made in this costly fabric. In the 16th century, the shirt as we now know it began to emerge, albeit heavily ornamented with lace and other fripperies at the wrist and around the neck. These were dispensed with in the post-French Revolution era, when simplicity of style began to be prized: Remember the Regency dandy Beau Brummell's axiom, "No perfumes but fine linen, plenty of it, and country washing."

The present form of plain, buttoned, and closely fitted cotton shirt only achieved widespread popularity in the 19th century as the urban middle class grew in number and needed to develop a practical wardrobe. The shirt with fastening cuffs and collar answered this requirement, although from around 1820 the collar was detachable, allowing it to be changed more frequently than the main part of the garment; this was because the collar most obviously showed dirt and signs of wear. In addition, it could be starched to retain stiffness while the rest of the shirt was left soft. The attached collar gradually grew in popularity in the first decades of the 20th century and is now the norm. But whatever its shape and fabric, a good shirt remains every gentleman's best friend; even today, to lose the shirt off one's back remains the ultimate symbol of shame.

Achieving the Perfect Shape

If you are not familiar with the manufacturer, it is always worth trying on a shirt before purchase, since there is now such a variety of construction methods that not all garments hang on the torso in the same way. You should learn that the key element is the yoke, namely the band of material that runs across the shoulder area and from which falls the body of the shirt. If this does not fit correctly then the rest of the garment won't either. While a couple of pleats are permitted on the back of the shirt (or a couple of darts for a more fitted style), the front should fall flat and fit snugly; the baggier the shirt, the less flattering to your frame. Breast pockets are problematic because they ruin the line of the shirt and so are best avoided; there are plenty of other places to store your glasses, credit cards, or mobile phone.

As regards length, there needs to be enough fabric that the shirt will not pop out of your waistband, but not so much material that it bunches when tucked into pants. While the untucked shirt is popular in certain circles, it should not be encouraged, because the result invariably looks untidy. It also implies that the man in question has put on weight and is trying to disguise evidence of this by not showing his waistband.

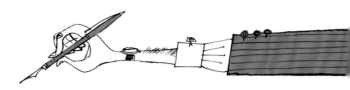

Sleeves and Cuffs

Sleeves should begin with armholes that fit well but are not so tight as to cut into the flesh, especially at the armpit. Likewise the main part of the sleeve should allow free movement but should not billow; when buying a new shirt it is worth seeing how it fits when worn beneath a sweater or jacket.

Sleeves should always be long enough to show sufficient cuff when hitting the wrist. In general, a cuff, whether single or double, should finish four and a half inches (11cm) from your thumb. When wearing any kind of jacket, approximately half an inch (1cm) of cuff must be visible.

The standard, or barrel, cuff is made from a single band of fabric and has one or two buttons to fasten it at the wrist. The French, or double, cuff folds back on itself and is fastened with cuff links, which should be visible when fastened and worn beneath a jacket.

Short-sleeved shirts never look entirely agreeable, perhaps because they suggest insufficient fabric was available to the manufacturer. If you want to adopt a casual appearance, better to roll up your sleeves.

In general, a cuff, whether single or double, should finish four and a half inches from your thumb

Collar Styles

Collars ought to fit but not to the point of threatening strangulation; ideally you should be able to fit two fingers under the collar at the side of the neck. The height and shape of the collar depend on taste but also on your own physique: a long neck, for example, responds better than does a short one to a high collar, especially one that fastens with a double button. Likewise the collar's shape will vary according to the size of tie-knot (or, indeed, lack of tie): As a rule, the wider the knot the more cutaway the collar. Unless wearing a button-down shirt, always use collar stays as they help to present a crisper appearance.

Among the commonly found collar styles is the Windsor, which is fairly widely spread—anything between four and six inches (10–15cm) between the collar points—and often found on business shirts. A narrower or smaller collar can look well but will only be able to accommodate thin ties.

The button-down collar is an American invention created by Brooks Brothers at the very end of the 19th century; it has not traveled much across the Atlantic because Europeans still prefer the Windsor collar. A variation of the button-down theme is the tab collar in which two narrow strips of fabric extend to the button point and are there linked behind a tie.

While most collars have pointed tips, occasionally one sees them with rounded ends: These are known as club collars. A shirt with a collar in a contrasting color to the main body of the shirt (most usually a white collar with striped body) is really a throwback to the days of the detachable collar. This style of shirt tends to be found in a business environment and looks out of place when worn without the accompaniment of a tie.

Fabric

Just as wool is by far the best fabric for suits, so cotton is ideal for shirting, with various forms of cotton poplin being most widely used for this purpose. Like wool, cotton is a natural material that is versatile, allows the skin to breathe, and takes and retains color well, but is also capable of surviving long-term use and regular washing.

Types of Weaves

A variety of weaves can be found in shirting cotton, the most ordinary being the plain weave where warp and weft (the horizontal and vertical threads combined to make cloth) are aligned to form a regular crisscross pattern. Oxford, which has a basketweave structure, provides a more hard-wearing weave than plain and so, too, does twill, which forms a pattern of diagonal parallel ribs by passing the weft over the warp thread. The twill weave's durability means it is also used for chino, denim, tweed, and gabardine. Satin weave imparts luster to the fabric and is therefore best kept for eveningwear shirts. Chambray is cotton woven with a colored warp and white weft, while flannelette is cotton that has been given a fur nap during the milling process to make it especially soft to the touch.

Alternatives to Cotton

Linen, which used to be the fabric of choice for gentlemen's shirts, is less widely used today except during summer months. It is vulnerable to wrinkling and can therefore quickly look untidy. Silk is the most luxurious of shirting materials but no longer tends to be much deployed for this purpose, except on occasion for eveningwear; even in heavier shantung, it is really too fine a fabric for day shirts.

Colors and Patterns

Every gentleman's wardrobe ought to hold several plain white shirts in various weights and weaves, all kept in pristine condition. You will find the white shirt invaluable, not least because it possesses universal adaptability to changing circumstances: A good white shirt looks as well with a suit as it does with jeans. Do not fret that a monochromatic shirt need be dull. There will be plenty of surface texture when it has been made with an Oxford or twill weave. Therefore, if you are planning to spend a reasonable sum of money on a couple of shirts, it is best to choose white. You will find they repay the investment.

As regards other colors, almost all are possible, but you ought to take your skin tone into account and be aware that not every shade will necessarily look well next to your face. As a general rule, during the daytime paler shades will suit you better, with darker ones kept for evenings. Likewise shirt patterns offer you an opportunity to play around with your wardrobe, although again a degree of moderation is recommended. Stripes look well in a business setting, as can some gingham, provided it is literally held in check. Other patterns, such as paisley, are best kept for informal times since they can very quickly impart the impression of frivolity to your appearance.

Don't be afraid to play around with your shirts, but, at the same time, bear in mind that mistakes can easily be made, especially if you are insufficiently aware of what best suits you and your style of dress.

If you are planning to spend a reasonable sum of money on a couple of shirts, it is best to choose white

Looking After Your Shirt

You should change your shirt, like your underwear, at least once a day. If you have an engagement in the evening, it is best to wear a clean shirt (and to shower before putting it on). Cotton is a resilient material and shirts can be washed in moderately hot water in order to make sure they are thoroughly cleaned; beforehand it is worth applying a specific stain removing detergent around the cuffs and collar as these areas are most vulnerable to dirt.

Never wash shirts in too hot a temperature as it may cause the fibers to shrink and the color to fade. Inevitably both shrinkage and fading are liable to happen over time, but there is no point in speeding up the process.

Avoiding Wrinkles

Hang the shirts to dry and iron them while they are still slightly damp as this will help to produce a smoother finish. In any case, you ought to use a steam iron for this purpose (or, alternatively, have close to hand a spray bottle filled with water). For a sharper look, use a spray starch on the sleeves and main body of the shirt (not on the collar as this could irritate your neck). When finished, hang your shirt again, with the top button closed to hold it in place. After a few hours, when it is completely dry, you can fold and store it away.

Try not to stack too many shirts on top of each other, because this might result in unwelcome wrinkling. Ideally, you should shake out a shirt and hang it up the night before it is being worn; this will reduce the wrinkles. Incidentally, the old trick of removing wrinkles by hanging a shirt within the steam of a hot running shower is still valid and particularly useful when you are traveling and without access to an iron.

CHAPTER 4

Knitwear

It is only in the past hundred years that knitwear has become a visible part of any gentleman's wardrobe. Previously, while a knitted garment might have been permissible when engaging in sport or as underwear, it was not usually worn in a social context. After World War I, however, long-established sartorial rules started to relax.

In the 1920s knitted waistcoats became fashionable and, in particular, the trend-setting Prince of Wales (later Duke of Windsor) took to wearing knitted tops in a Fair Isle pattern while playing golf: hence their rise in acceptability. Nevertheless, note how the association with sport still remained, as it did with V-neck sweaters carrying a particular sporting club's colors around the neck and hem. Only in the 1930s did knitwear make the full transition from sports arena to everyday environment. Even so, it was very much a casual style, meant to be worn only inside the home and on informal occasions.

Sleeveless sweaters worn with tweed jackets became popular, as did V-necks with the diamond pattern known as Argyle. It took another world war before crewneck and turtleneck sweaters, known as polo-necks in the UK, began to be seen in public, initially worn by a generation of avant-garde artists and musicians before being taken up by the general population. Cardigans

> *Cashmere is taken from the coat of a goat of the same name and is a byword for comfort*

likewise gradually grew in popularity during the postwar decades. By the 1960s knitwear had become entirely mainstream, taken up by designers such as the Italians Tai and Rosita Missoni who gave sweaters a fashion fillip. So it remains to this day and now every gentleman is likely to own a number of pieces of knitwear. At all times it serves a dual purpose: to provide warmth and to add style. If either of these functions is not met, then the knit in question has not done its job.

Choosing Materials

Different animal fibers can be used in the manufacture of knitwear, the most widespread being lamb's-wool. Sheared from sheep up to seven months old, it is light in weight and easy to spin into yarn.

The Merino sheep is agreed to produce some of the very finest and softest wool, while Shetland sheep yield wool that is inclined to be coarse but resilient. There are various other yarns used in knitwear such as vicuña and alpaca, both of which are taken from species of South American llama and are renowned for their luxurious softness. So, too, is angora, which comes from a species of rabbit bred since the 18th century for this purpose. Cashmere is taken from the coat of a goat of the same name and is a byword for comfort and cost, not surprisingly since the average annual yield per goat is only five ounces (around 150 grams). Cashmere manages to be both light and warm, and this combination—when added to its inherently tactile qualities—explains the fiber's abiding popularity in the manufacture of quality knitwear. Any and all of these natural fibers are acceptable for knitwear. Artificial fibers are not.

The Right Style

What style knitwear you choose depends on both the occasion and your own physique. Sweaters are still predominantly associated

with informality and rarely seen in the average workplace. Therefore they are not, as a rule, worn with suits. However, if you are going to do so you will find your jacket's shape is least disrupted by the inclusion of a lightweight sleeveless top; bulkier items will distort the whole profile. In some creative professions, crewnecks and turtlenecks are found worn with suits; again, lighter weights will work best.

Outside the office, at the weekend, and on vacation you should choose a style that best suits your body shape. A V-neck sweater will elongate the torso, especially if it has vertical bands incorporated into the knit. It is therefore flattering to short men. If you have a long, thin neck then the crewneck—which has a round neckline finishing well below the Adam's apple—will not be especially flattering. On the other hand, a turtleneck (which is useful for concealing the wrinkly skin of this area) should be avoided by men with short necks as it only emphasizes this aspect of their physiology.

Advice on Fit

Your knitwear ought to fit comfortably but properly. As with suit jackets, many men are inclined to wear sweaters too big for them, with the result that they look untidy. Avoid knitwear that bags at the midriff, otherwise it will give the erroneous impression that you have a paunch. On the other hand, if you are somewhat thickset, don't wear a tight sweater: the outline of your stomach straining to escape its confines will not win admirers. Men carrying additional weight should consider cardigans since these have the merit of being left partially or wholly unbuttoned.

Acceptable Patterns

Aside from classic Fair Isle and Argyle, it is recommended that you steer well clear of patterns in knitwear; novelty in this area is rarely carried off with élan (remember Colin Firth's seasonal Christmas sweater in *Bridget Jones's Diary*?). The merit of vertical stripes has already been mentioned. Horizontal stripes can likewise deceive the eye, in this instance by making a thin man look broader, although with some knitwear they can also make him look like an aspiring French sailor. Within reasonable boundaries, do regard knitwear as an opportunity of introducing color into your dress, especially if the rest of your outfit is sober in design and cut.

Do regard knitwear as an opportunity of introducing color into your outfit

Caring For Your Knitwear

The natural fibers used in its construction mean that all knitwear will stretch somewhat when worn—and correspondingly shrink when washed. Learn how to take off your knitwear properly (that is, using two hands and from the bottom waistband up over your head) as this will preserve its shape better. Always fold your sweater after use, preferably incorporating tissue paper. All knitwear should be washed, ideally by hand and at a low temperature, before being laid flat to dry. Never tumble dry your sweaters as this will cause the fibers to shrink and will distort the garment's shape.

CHAPTER 5

Ties

Even though today it serves no practical purpose, the tie remains an essential element in any gentleman's wardrobe. In its present guise this item of clothing can be traced back to the cravats worn by men from the mid-17th century onward; these took the place of ruffs, which had previously been the preferred style of neck attire. Over the next 150-odd years cravats changed from an elaborate confection of lace to a simple folded piece of white linen carefully knotted below the chin. A version of this survives to the present day in the form of the stock worn by horsemen when out hunting.

The elegance of the cravat reached its peak in the early 1800s: Regency dandy Beau Brummell is supposed to have spent entire mornings perfecting the finish of his cravat before he was ready to emerge from his home. However, during the second half of the 19th century the cravat in turn began to be superseded by the tie as we now know it: a plain strip of fabric wound once around the neck and then tied in a knot at the front from which two ends descend toward the waist.

What Your Tie Says about You

The tie has come to have an unexpected function, its objective being not to keep the body warm but to send out a signal about the wearer's place in society. Essentially ties are symbols, not least of conformity—hence an inevitable reluctance on the part of the young and would-be rebellious to wear them. Hence, too, the popularity of ties carrying emblems or crests, or particular sequences of stripes: These indicate the wearer is a member of a specific group or club. The phrase "old school tie" has become a figure of speech denoting the merits of belonging to a particular caste. In addition, ties are deemed to signify respectability, making them a requisite feature of business dress. Ties are not easy to produce and are complex works of engineering that should be admired. Finally, ties have developed in line with the modern suit and shirt, and therefore naturally harmonize with them. For all these reasons, you ought to have a number of ties in your wardrobe.

Fabric Selection

As a rule ties are made of silk and certainly no synthetic materials should be used to produce them. The silk must be woven and it is easy to detect whether this is the case by looking at a tie's pattern, which ought never to be printed. Different weights and weaves of silk—such as twill and poplin—will produce varying styles of material for use in a tie and this in turn has an impact on the knot used when tying it. Bear in mind these factors when purchasing a tie. For a more relaxed approach, consider knitted ties, either in silk or cashmere. These work well in rural environments when combined with a sleeveless sweater and tweed jacket; in such scenarios a woven silk tie can look too urban.

Color and Pattern

Ties permit a man to express something of his personality even when the rest of what he is wearing suggests anonymous uniformity. For this reason, you need not shirk away from bold colors and patterns, provided they complement rather than conflict with your shirt and suit. Relish the opportunity to demonstrate individual taste through your choice of tie while remaining within the bounds of good taste. Think in terms of classic designs like diagonal stripes or paisley patterns rather than novelty. Avoid "jokey" ties or anything intended to be funny, or the laugh will inevitably be on you. And obviously you should never wear a tie connected with any institution, such as a club or school, unless you really have links with it.

Tying Your Tie

In Oscar Wilde's 1893 play *A Woman of No Importance*, the droll Lord Illingworth proclaims, "A well-tied tie is the first serious step in life." It transpires there are a surprisingly large number of ways to tie a tie. In 1999, two Cambridge University physicists, Thomas Fink and Yong Mao, published a book called *The 85 Ways to Tie a Tie: The Science and Aesthetics of Tie Knots* in which they listed all the possible ways of tying a tie, but then picked out thirteen, including four classics—the four-in-hand, the Pratt, the

Relish the opportunity to demonstrate individual taste through your choice of tie while remaining within the bounds of good taste

half-Windsor, and the Windsor—which stood out as aesthetically satisfying. Most men tend to use the four-in-hand, which is relatively easy to learn and also looks well with all widths and weights of fabric. The Windsor dates from the 1930s and takes its name from the Duke of Windsor, who then liked a broad knot; the half-Windsor is a variation on this theme.

Correct Length

If you prefer to learn how to tie a variety of knots such as the Windsor and half-Windsor, several websites offer guidance on the subject and provide helpful illustrations for each stage of the process.

Be careful to wear your tie neither too long nor too short: It should stop just short of your belt. The narrower tail should be concealed behind the front and if there is a loop at the rear of the latter use this to tuck away the former. Clip-on ties, obviously, are never to be countenanced.

Looking After Your Ties

As with the rest of your wardrobe, if you take care of a tie you will find it gives longer and better service. Never wear a tie on consecutive days but allow at least 24 hours for it to recover its shape. Ideally you should not hang your ties (most especially if they are knitted) but roll them up from the thin end and then store them flat. If you must hang your tie collection, buy a hanger designed for this function. To remove wrinkles in a tie, hold it up before the steam of a kettle (making sure the entire item does not become wet). Avoid ironing ties because it often flattens the natural bounce of the fabric used in their manufacture.

Ties are prone to become stained, particularly with food. These

How to Tie a Four-in-Hand

1. A four-in-hand is very straightforward. Start by hanging the tie around your neck with the widest section to the right and falling longer than the narrow part.

2. Pass the wide end over the front of the narrow end to the left, then under it to the right.

3. Pass the wide end over the front of the narrow end to the left once more.

4. Now pass the wide end behind the semi-formed knot and pull it up toward your chin.

5. Finally, pass the wide end between the outer layer of the knot and the layer directly behind it, before pulling the tip of the tie through.

6. Hold the narrow end firmly and then tighten the knot until it is sitting firmly but comfortably at the top of your shirt.

marks should be removed as soon as possible, preferably with an appropriate spot remover. Test the product's efficacy and potential risk to the fabric beforehand, using an inconspicuous section of the tie at the back. Always dab a stain rather than rubbing it which could affect the color of the material. Likewise do not wash ties since the nature of their construction (more complicated than you might imagine) is likely to mean different sections have different shrink rates.

Bow Ties

The bow tie is a prerequisite of evening dress. In recent years some men have taken to wearing a regular knotted black tie in its place but this makes a very poor second, rather like serving sparkling wine instead of Champagne. If you are wearing the full formality of evening tails, then the bow tie, like your wing-collared shirt, ought to be made of white cotton piqué. When donning a tuxedo, or dinner jacket, your tie will be of black ribbed silk. Colored ties in the evening are a sartorial solecism made even worse when they are accompanied by matching cummerbunds or waistcoats. Evening bow ties must always be either white or black, depending on the circumstances; nothing else is acceptable.

Sadly, few men now wear bow ties during the day and they are certainly not part of contemporary business attire, as was the case even until half a century ago. With a tweed jacket or a

How to Tie a Bow Tie

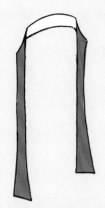

1. Drape the tie around your neck leaving one end an inch or two longer than the other.

2. Cross the longer end over the shorter end.

3. Using the longer end, wrap it around the shorter end and tie a simple knot.

4. Hold up the longer end with your thumb and forefinger by your face so that it is out of the way. With your other hand, form the short end into a bow.

5. Let the longer end fall down over the front of the bow, which you must now hold in position. Grasp the longer end and force half of it through the gap which is behind the bow.

6. After pushing the bow through from one side, pull on the other side and thus tighten the knot before straightening all the layers so that they form a neat bow. If any part is longer than the rest or skewed, gently tug or twist it so that the whole tie looks neat.

Does it need to be said that pre-tied bows are absolutely beyond the pale?

cardigan, a paisley pattern bow tie can provide a nice touch, intimating a kind of relaxed formality. For daywear, patterned rather than plain bows are indubitably preferable and suggestive of an earlier, less frenetic era than our own.

Does it need to be said that pre-tied bows are absolutely beyond the pale? It is astonishing how many men who regard themselves as practical and competent to change a tire or investigate the intricacies of computer components are rendered helpless when required to tie a bow around their necks. As a means of enticing a woman to stand immediately behind and put her arms around you, this display of dependency has a certain charm but what if there is no such woman around? As with other aspects of adulthood, self-reliance is required when it comes to tying a bow.

CHAPTER 6

Shoes

It used to be said that hotel concierges could judge the financial status of their guests by the condition of the latter's shoes: The scruffier their footwear, the less they were deemed to be worth (and therefore liable to receive a proportionately poorer reception). But the casual shoes favored by many of today's new billionaires give no indication of their immense wealth, so that rule has had to be discarded.

Even if you can no longer estimate the size of a man's bank balance by how he is shod, you can still gain a fair understanding of how much pride he takes in himself and his appearance by the state of his shoes. Scruffy footwear suggests a slovenly attitude. A pair of clean, well-polished shoes, on the other hand, indicates orderliness and an appreciation of standards.

Getting the Right Size

It is worth spending as much as you can on your shoes, not least because they offer vital support as you walk and stand your way through the average day. Rather like the bespoke suit, if your bank balance allows you to commission a pair of custom-made shoes, then you should do so. Constructed to fit you like a second skin, with due maintenance they will last the rest of your lifetime. Should such expenditure be beyond your means, at least take the trouble to have your feet correctly measured and thereafter only buy shoes that are the right size. Disregard any sales assistant who assures you a shoe will stretch or become softer with wear—it ought to be comfortable from the first occasion.

Most men find that their right foot is fractionally larger than the left, so always try on the right shoe first. If it fits properly, more than likely so too will the left. Always scrupulously examine shoes before you buy them, paying particular attention to how well the uppers and soles have been stitched together since this is often an area where standards are allowed to slip.

Acceptable Materials

Other than sports shoes and sneakers, all your shoes must be made of an animal hide, most commonly calf although there is also a rich leather called Cordovan made from the flat muscle beneath the hide on a horse's rump. Hide will respond best to your own skin, subtly expanding and contracting as do the feet they encase, allowing your feet to breathe and absorbing any excess perspiration that passes through the hide before being dispersed into the outside air. Occasionally other hides, such as buckskin (from deer) and those taken from reptiles or birds like ostrich, are used for the manufacture of shoes, but the result is inclined to be rather flashy and attention-seeking.

Leather or Suede?

Until the 1920s suede was viewed with suspicion but then, as in so many other areas of men's fashion, it was espoused by the future Duke of Windsor and thus acquired a degree of respectability.

> *Leather tends to look better in a formal or professional environment, while suede is more suited to casual times*

Leather tends to look better in a formal or professional environment, while suede is more suited to casual times like weekends at home. Patent leather should only be used for evening shoes.

Black or Brown?

It used to be a strict rule that gentlemen never wore brown shoes in town; they were kept for the country. However, this no longer applies. Paradoxically, black shoes often look out of place in a rural setting, so keep brown shoes to hand (or rather, to foot) whenever in the countryside. Ideally your wardrobe should contain several pairs of shoes in both colors.

Can you wear shoes of a color other than black or brown? Certainly not in leather, but a colored suede can look stylish for casual loafers, especially in warmer climates.

A Style to Suit the Occasion

The Oxford is the stalwart of shoes, a basic, plain style characterized by the way in which the lace eyelets are stitched beneath the upper (or vamp, as it is known). The Derby, on the other hand, has its lace eyelets stitched on top of the vamp.

The wing-tip is distinguished from the Oxford by the shape of the toe cap which instead of running straight across the bridge of the shoe spreads in a fashion not unlike that of the open wings of a bird.

Oxfords work well with a business suit and are certainly the preferred style in a professional environment.

Brogues can be worn with a business suit, but as befits their Scottish origins look exceptionally good with tweeds

The brogue originated in the Scottish Highlands and is identifiable by the elaborate series of tiny holes punched across sections of the shoe upper which is also decorated with double-stitched seams. The difference between a half- and a full-brogue is that the former's perforation and double-stitching are confined to the front section of the shoe. Brogues can be worn with a business suit, but as befits their Scottish origins look exceptionally good with tweeds.

The monk shoe does not have laces but instead a strap passes across the instep and is fastened by a buckle. It is the descendant of the 17th-century buckled shoe but only emerged in its present form in the 1930s. The monk shoe is extremely versatile and combines well with both formal and casual clothes.

The loafer (or moccasin) likewise first appeared during the 1930s and originated in Norway where it was made by fishermen. Obviously at first it was a somewhat rough-and-ready product but soon underwent refinement in accordance with increased popularity. It now comes in several variants such as the tassel loafer, the kiltie (which has a fringe across the instep), and the penny-loafer, so called because during the 1950s there was a fad for lodging pennies in the little diamond-shaped cutout at the top. In the mid-1960s Gucci added a metal strap across the front of its loafers in the shape of a horse's snaffle bit and this has since been much emulated. Loafers, depending on their style and finish,

Looking After Your Shoes

There is no reason why a pair of shoes should not continue to provide sturdy service for many years—no reason other than your failure to take as much care of them as they have of you. Follow these rules to keep your shoes in a good state of repair:

* Never wear shoes on consecutive days. Allow them to rest and recover from being worn.

* Always use shoe trees when they are resting as this will help immeasurably in preserving their correct shape.

* If your shoes get wet, stuff them with newspaper which will absorb the excess moisture. Change the paper a couple of times to make sure all the water has been soaked up.

* Regularly check the heels of your shoes and have the rubber of these replaced as soon as it starts to show evidence of being worn down. Likewise the soles will need to be periodically repaired.

* When traveling, pack your shoes inside individual shoe bags. This will ensure they do not get scratched or leave marks on other items.

* Above all, clean and polish your shoes on a weekly basis using a cream polish, which will nourish and protect the leather. Ideally you should apply the polish and then leave it for a while to be absorbed into the shoe before buffing it to a high sheen. Any dirt should be removed beforehand with a damp sponge.

* Suede shoes can also be maintained with the aid of a brush intended for this purpose, using short strokes in the direction of the nap to remove any dirt.

Loafers, depending on their style and finish, are sufficiently adaptable to be worn in almost every circumstance

are sufficiently adaptable to be worn in almost every circumstance.

The boat or deck shoe, as its name indicates, began life on board a seagoing vessel where the combination of nonslip soles and water-repellent leather made it invaluable. No longer confined offshore, deck shoes are now found on land but are strictly for casualwear.

The pump is a shoe designed for evening wear. It is entirely plain and low-heeled, made from either polished or patent hide and most commonly is slip-on.

Chelsea boots are really the only kind of boots that can be worn when not playing sport. They derive from a 19th-century fitted, ankle-high jodhpur boot and have elasticized sidings. In the 1960s they became highly fashionable and have remained popular ever since. They are casual items and not suited to the workplace.

CHAPTER 7

Socks and Underwear

Just because it's not on public view, you shouldn't
assume the state of your underwear is
unimportant. The female equivalent used to be
known as foundation garments, and that's how you
should view these items: as providing a sound base
for your clothes. Likewise, young girls were once
told by their mothers always to wear clean
underwear in case they were hit by a bus and taken
to hospital. You needn't imagine such a drastic
scene but there will come times when you're
grateful to have put on decent underwear that day.

Socks

All of us have an abundance of socks in our wardrobe, ideally kept
in matching pairs: The riddle of the missing sock will be familiar
to every man and defies explanation. There are really only a handful
of rules to follow when it comes to these items, and none is
too arduous.

Fabrics used for the making of socks were once entirely natural,
such as silk, cashmere, wool, and cotton. These are still employed but
most often today mixed with a certain percentage of a man-made

Colored and patterned socks can enhance an outfit provided they harmonize with it and do not upstage it

material like polyamide, which greatly increases the durability of the finished item. This is especially important for socks which can otherwise suffer the affliction of becoming speedily worn out and then ruined by the emergence of holes at heel and toe. So for once a degree of man-made fiber is to be recommended, but not more than 20 percent.

Silk is best for evening socks, being lighter and finer; cashmere is especially luxurious (but not terribly hard-wearing); wool is generally warmer than cotton, the latter being best kept for summer socks. Merino wool is the ideal for everyday socks.

Color and Pattern

For office and formal occasions, your socks will be dark and without any knitted ribbing. Ribbed socks are for weekends and sports attire. Your socks should always be at least one shade darker than your trousers and, off the tennis court or sports field, ought never to be white. Colored and patterned socks can enhance an outfit provided they harmonize with what else is being worn and do not try to upstage it. Beware of novelty socks—you'll find the novelty wears out faster than the socks.

Sock Length

Wear a sock of sufficient length so that when you sit down no calf is exposed. There are few more unattractive spectacles than a band of pale flesh between bottom of pant leg and top of sock. Garters used to be needed in order to keep the top of a sock in place but elastication has done away with this; just make sure your socks retain their elasticity and do not end up crumpled around the ankle.

Looking After Your Socks

As with other knitwear, due care ought to be taken when washing socks. This is best done at a low temperature to avoid both shrinkage and color loss.

Regularly check your socks for holes: They can appear with startling ease and a man with a hole in his hosiery is a sorry sight. The days of sock mushrooms (used for darning repairs) are long over, but if you want to increase the chances of a sock's longevity, keep your toenails short and your ankle smooth. While it is impossible to guarantee against losing one half of a pair, the danger will be reduced if you fold the top of each set of socks over one another before putting them away.

The riddle of the missing sock will be familiar to every man and defies explanation

Underwear

The function of underwear is first and foremost hygienic: to act as a protective layer between your body and its secretions and your outer

garments. In cold weather it also provides a layer of warmth. Any other advantage is supplementary, so you should choose underwear for its ability to perform a sanitary function. This means, above all else, making sure it is made from a natural fiber, most commonly cotton, although, as with socks, a small element of man-made fiber—such as Lycra—in the mix is permissible, not least because it ensures a snugger fit. Linen and silk are more expensive and do not necessarily do a better job than cotton. In an era of central heating, wool

underwear is redundant. Men's underwear at the start of the 20th century was usually the one-piece set of long johns encasing an entire form from neck to wrist and ankle. This shrank and separated into two separate pieces, one for the upper body, one for the lower.

Undershirts and T-shirts

The undershirt, or vest, which was widely worn during those early decades, suffered an irreversible decline in popularity after Clark Gable removed his shirt in the 1934 Frank Capra film *It Happened*

What style your underwear takes—briefs, boxers, fitted shorts—is a matter of personal predilection

One Night and revealed he was wearing nothing beneath. Thereafter undershirts have been afflicted with the notion that they are old-fashioned. Their place in a man's wardrobe has been largely supplanted by the T-shirt which was popularized in the 1950s by another film actor, Marlon Brando. While it may be tempting to dispense with anything beneath your shirt, wearing some kind of undershirt or T retains merit, not least because it will absorb the evidence should you perspire during the day.

Boxers or Briefs?

Some men are likewise attracted to the notion of going "commando," that is, not bothering with any lower underwear. For reasons of hygiene this is to be discouraged. What style your underwear takes—briefs, boxers, fitted shorts—is a matter of personal predilection since it is unlikely to be seen by the majority of people you meet. It has sometimes been proposed that a man's fecundity can be adversely affected by too-tight clothing, but there is no absolute evidence proving this to be so. Ultimately, comfort ought to be your guide. Plain colors and an absence of pattern are probably preferable, but if you want to use your underwear as an opportunity to express individuality it has the advantage of being a discreet manifestation.

What can absolutely not be disputed is the importance of keeping your underwear clean and changing it at least once a day. Under no circumstances can this rule be breached.

CHAPTER 8

Accessories

Accessories should be considered the finishing touches to an outfit, not critical to your overall appearance but capable of lifting you from the realm of smartly dressed to the heights of impeccably turned out. Remember that it's the little things that make all the difference and accessorize accordingly.

———•———

Gloves

Gloves used to be an everyday part of the gentleman's wardrobe. They were worn on almost every occasion: when either riding or walking in public, as well as at the theater or going to church. One of the functions of gloves in earlier times was the protection of hands, both from the cold and from dirt and germs. They can still serve the same purpose and ought to remain an integral part of your daily wardrobe, except, of course, when the weather grows too warm.

Acceptable Materials

In winter, for heat it is recommended that you wear gloves lined in cashmere, which has the advantage of being deliciously soft. In spring, change these for gloves lined in silk.

Your gloves should be of the finest leather affordable. Originating from South American wild hogs, peccary is the rarest and most luxurious leather used for gloves. More normally hair-sheep leather—which, as its name indicates, comes from sheep that grow hair rather than wool—is employed, because it combines suppleness and strength with softness. Deerskin is especially tough but it is heavier and more rugged in appearance. Cheaper gloves are often made from cowhide and goatskin.

Caring for Your Gloves

As with every other item in your wardrobe, be sure to buy gloves in the right size. Too small and they will pinch, too big and they will not necessarily keep your hands as warm as ought to be the case.

Just like the hands they contain, gloves suffer from rough treatment and benefit from care. After a day's wear, always gently stretch each finger and the main body to restore its original shape. Lay the gloves flat, and store them in a dry place (damp will cause them to develop mold) and inside a cloth cover. Lightly sponge them with a moist cloth to remove any dirt and periodically treat them with something that will improve the leather and keep it supple; even petroleum jelly or a waterless hand moisturizer will serve the purpose. Rub this into the leather while wearing the gloves and then wipe off any excess with a dry cloth.

Umbrellas

The umbrella serves an entirely practical purpose but that does not mean it should not also be aesthetically pleasing. Initially an object of ridicule when it first made an appearance in 18th-century England, the umbrella proved so useful that it became an invaluable accessory, particularly in damper climes. Toward the close of the

Black is the only acceptable color for umbrella fabric

19th century, a tightly rolled umbrella had begun to replace the walking stick as the object carried by every respectable gentleman.

In an urban setting, a plain black umbrella remains the best choice, preferably one with a simple handle of stainless steel topped by either polished wood or stitched leather. Black is the only acceptable color for umbrella fabric. Until the 1940s this used to be made of fine silk, which was subject to discoloration and rotting when damp. Since then, however, a number of durable nylons have been developed and have now largely replaced silk. The collapsible, tote-style umbrella is extremely useful as it does not take up as much space, but is often of inferior manufacture and not as robust as the more traditional stick. Golf umbrellas belong on the golf course; in towns and cities they take up too much room on the sidewalk and anyone carrying one in these places shows a selfish lack of consideration for his fellow men and women. Umbrellas displaying slogans or advertisements turn their owners into walking billboards.

If you have used your umbrella in the rain, always open it when you get home and allow the body to dry out before furling it up again. This will ensure a longer life for the item.

Jewelry

As far as men and jewelry are concerned, less is definitely best. Anything you wear should be simple in form and design, with minimal decoration and no overt evidence of expense.

With regard to rings, a plain band in gold or platinum on the third finger of your left hand is permissible as a statement of marriage. If you have a family crest, a gold signet ring may be worn on the little finger of the left hand: the seal should face outward to enable a wax impression to be taken without removing the ring. No other rings should be worn.

Any jewelry that involves piercing the flesh is not permissible. Likewise all bracelets and necklaces.

Cuff links and Tie Pins

For double-cuff shirts, cuff links are a necessity. Once more they should be made of a precious metal, most often silver or gold, and should be as unostentatious as possible. The classic link involves two bars or studs linked by a chain but the alternative link by bar is also fine. With evening wear, links incorporating gems can look well, provided the stones are not too big. Cuff links made from colored silk knots can be worn with a shirt during the day, but precious metals are preferable at night. It is worth building up a small collection of links, to vary according to circumstance.

Shirt studs, again sometimes incorporating gems but more often with black enameled fronts, are deemed perfectly respectable with evening dress.

Tie pins and clips used to be in common usage but are not much seen today. Older examples often featured gemstones or enameled images but these now look unnecessarily fussy. If you are going to use something to keep your tie in place, make it as low-key as possible.

A Simple Timepiece

Your watch, like your shoes, provides information about you and your character. A cheap watch will make you look cheap. On the other hand, showiness here is to be avoided; although your watch might have cost a great deal of money, this should not be apparent. So no loud diamonds, no superfluous dials and buttons, no heavily ornamented wrist bands (the last of these should be in plain dark leather). Leave ostentation to drug dealers and rap stars, and let quiet good taste be your guiding principle in the selection of a watch and indeed all other pieces of jewelry.

Belts

Obviously the primary intent of a belt is to keep your pants from falling to the ground (as seen in a thousand comedy films), but they also help to complete an outfit, especially if the pants you are wearing have belt loops; in the absence of a belt these can look empty and gaping. Accordingly, you should always wear a belt if your pants are designed for this purpose.

The color of your belt should match that of your shoes and likewise be of leather. The belt's width should be in the region of an inch and a half (4cm) and its tongue should extend about three inches (7.5cm) beyond the buckle but not much more.

For business and evening attire, a plain buckle is the only option acceptable. With casual pants and especially jeans, a decorative buckle can be worn—but keep the ornamentation within reasonable limits.

CHAPTER 9

Formal Occasions

By their nature formal occasions do not encourage spontaneity or expressions of individuality in matters of dress. There are well-established codes to be followed and unless you particularly yearn to be noticed it is best to adhere to them. Besides, as a demonstration of personal rebellion your failure to wear the correct clothes to a wedding can hardly be deemed radical. Better to adhere to the established rules and find another opportunity for a display of your seditious character.

Evening Wear

While men have a limited choice of outfit for evening functions compared with women, there is still a margin for error when planning your outfit. Men's evening dress can be summarized as falling into two categories: the dresscoat and the tuxedo, also known as a dinner jacket. Consider carefully the purpose of the night's engagement and ensure that you dress appropriately.

The Dress Coat

The white tie dress code, also known as full evening dress, is, and has been for more than a century, the most formal style of male costume, worn only on grand occasions such as a formal ball or gala evening.

As such, its components are firmly regulated and do not admit of variation. The centerpiece of the ensemble is the black evening tailcoat—the dress coat—made of a lightweight mohair with silk facings, cut away horizontally at the front. The reason for this style lies in its late 18th-century origins, when a coat was needed that could be worn by men when riding. In its current incarnation, the dress coat is a descendant of an item once worn during both day and night toward the close of the 18th century. For day wear it was supplanted around the middle of the 19th century by the frock coat and this in turn gave way to the morning coat, which is still worn today for some government and civic events. In Britain and Europe it is also worn at formal weddings and so forth. In the Regency era, trousers or breeches did not match the dress coat, but since the latter became exclusively the preserve of evening wear, it has been customary for both to be made from the same cloth, and always to be black.

In cut, the coat is waist-length at front and sides, but at the rear has two long swallowtails falling to the knee. Remember them before sitting down—rather than crushing them on the seat, you should separate the tails, one to either side of your chair. Since the 1870s the coat has been double-breasted with two rows of buttons. However, these are only decorative as the coat does not fasten. Unlike its ancestor, it has no external pockets other than one at the breast.

The accompanying pants, in the same fabric, will have a fish-tail back, indicating that they are to be held in place by suspenders

An evening shirt will be plain white and will be accompanied by a white bow tie. No other color is acceptable

(known as braces in Britain) rather than a belt. Down the outer seams runs a single or double stripe of silk braid.

Your shirt will be plain white with a stiff front of cotton piqué and a wing collar. This will be accompanied by a white bow tie, also of cotton piqué. No other color should be countenanced. Likewise the waistcoat will be of white cotton piqué, cut low and double-breasted with a slim shawl collar. Its bottom should not extend lower than does the front of your dress coat, in order to present an unbroken black silhouette.

Socks will be to the knee and black, preferably silk or else fine merino wool. Your footwear will likewise be black and if possible patent leather. Should you find yourself much in demand for formal evening occasions, it is worth acquiring a pair of plain black pumps (also known as court shoes) with bows of grossgrain. The only other accessories permissible are a plain white linen handkerchief in the breast pocket and/or a boutonniere in your buttonhole. Men in possession of military medals and other similar decorations also wear them on their dress coats. Every now and then someone will appear with a top hat which is also a traditional part of formal evening wear but rarely seen today. If you intend to carry one, it should be black, made of silk, and collapsible—a relic from the days when gentlemen wore such hats to the opera and had to store them under their chair. A dark coat and gloves, together with silk scarf, should be worn for protection of your clothes if you are traveling.

The Dinner Jacket

Although the dinner jacket is called a tuxedo in North America, the word tuxedo is also often used there for any tailcoat, so the term dinner jacket is used here to distinguish between them. It is worn for evening events where the dress code is black tie.

The dinner jacket is of far more recent vintage than the dress coat and its rise testifies to the increasingly casual nature of men's clothing over the past century. The dinner jacket can be traced back to a visit made in 1886 by the wealthy New Yorker James Potter to the Prince of Wales (later Edward VII) at Sandringham, England. Seemingly when Potter asked his host about a dresscode he was sent to the London tailor Henry Poole & Co, who provided him with a suit similar to the smoking jackets made to the Prince's specifications for the past quarter-century; this was, in effect, a dinner jacket and trousers. Returning to the United States, Potter wore his dinner suit to the club attached to Tuxedo Park, then one of New York's most fashionable residential districts. It quickly acquired a following among the club's members and from this derives its American name, the tuxedo.

Initially, dinner jackets were seen only at home or in a club setting, while the dress coat continued to be worn on more public and formal occasions. However, from the 1920s onward it began to replace the dress coat and is now the standard male option for evening dress. Although open to a certain degree of flexibility, nevertheless some rules are best applied when wearing a dinner

The rise of the dinner jacket testifies to the increasingly casual nature of men's clothing over the last century

jacket. The classic style for jackets is that they be made of light mohair with ribbed satin facings on a shawl lapel (derived from smoking jackets) or peaked lapel (from dress coats). Either single- or double-breasted is acceptable but the latter will accentuate any excess weight so only the slim should choose this style. Jackets should be either black or blue-black. If you wear another color, usually in velvet, it is classified as a smoking jacket, which in full fig will have a shawl collar and be fastened by silk froggings. Smoking jackets, while perfectly fine for a semiformal dinner in a private house, should not be worn to a public occasion.

The white dinner jacket originated in hot climates and traditionally was never seen in England: for a long time men who wore such a garment outside the tropics were regarded with suspicion. Although this is no longer the case, a white jacket will best be kept for summer evenings. Its color is not so much white as a pale ivory and it has a lapel, usually shawl, made of the same light fabric.

Regardless of the color of your jacket, the accompanying pants should always be black and made from light mohair with a single silk or satin braid running the length of the outer seams. Traditionally the pants are flat-fronted (that is, without pleats) and held in place by suspenders (braces), which are then concealed either by a waistcoat or by the jacket.

As for the waistcoat, it used to be backless, low-cut, and, whether single- or double-breasted, with no more than three rows of buttons. However, since men began to remove their jackets during the course of a long evening (something that never used to occur), evening waistcoats have acquired a full back and they close higher on the chest in the manner of their daytime equivalents.

In recent years cummerbunds have become increasingly popular. These items derive from military dress uniform in colonial India where they were worn as an alternative to the waistcoat. Made from the same material as the bow tie and jacket facings, a cummerbund is worn with its pleats facing upward. Of late there has been a trend for cummerbunds (and matching bow ties) to be in a variety of colors and patterns, but this has the disadvantage of spoiling evening dress's elegant formality and is unacceptable to the purist.

The same is true for the accompanying shirt which should always be white, of the finest cotton, and have a turn-down collar; wing collars are worn only with the dress coat. The shirt front can be pleated or plain and, if it does not have a fly-front placket, should fasten with a series of shirt studs—these ought to be made either of silver or, possibly, gold and feature mother-of-pearl, onyx, or some other semi-precious stone. In such circumstances, you should have matching cuff links to close your cuffs.

A plain black ribbed silk bow tie, matching the lapel facings of the jacket, will be worn at the neck. This should be self- and not pre-tied. There are two common styles of ties: the butterfly wing, which has a central bulge and flares at the end, and the bat wing, which has parallel sides. The second of these forms a smaller and neater bow, and is the preferable option. Beginning among actors and then emulated by their admirers, there has been a fondness to wear a regular black tie instead of a bow tie with a dinner jacket. Aside from suggesting you are an off-duty funeral director, this style also implies the inability to tie a bow. Neither implication does much for your credibility.

Socks will be black, of silk or fine merino wool, and knee-length, while shoes—also black—are either patent or highly polished Oxfords. The only acceptable accessories are a well-starched white linen handkerchief in the breast pocket and possibly a small flower as boutonniere.

Weddings

If you are attending a wedding, the invitation card may specify a dress code for the occasion. This is likely to fall into the following categories: a business (or lounge) suit; a dinner jacket; or morning dress.

The Business Suit and Dinner Jacket

The first of these requires you to wear a matching jacket and pants, together with shirt and tie. Fabric, color, and so forth will depend on the time of year, the weather, and your personal taste, although it is never a good idea to be better dressed than the groom (or the bride). The dinner jacket will be a black tuxedo and trousers with white shirt and black tie, as described on pages 76–78.

Morning Dress

Morning dress—which, despite its name, can be worn at any time during the day—is the most formal daytime dress code and is worn in Britain and Europe at formal weddings. The morning coat is a variation on the dress coat and derives from the same era, the late 18th/early 19th century, when a tailcoat cut for ease while riding became the norm.

The main element of morning dress is the morning coat, sometimes called a cutaway. It is single-breasted with the front meeting at one button in the middle, after which it curves gently

away to conclude in a pair of knee-length tails at the rear, two ornamental buttons featuring here on the waist seam. In color it can be either black or Oxford gray and made of herringbone wool, with pointed lapels of the same fabric. The accompanying pants are usually in a thin gray and black stripe (very occasionally these are checked), with one or two pleats at the waistband; as with the dress coat, here, too, suspenders (braces) rather than a belt are worn to support the pants and ensure there is no gap between their top and the bottom of the waistcoat.

Traditionally the morning coat waistcoat was gray, black, or buff (a pale yellow-brown color), but of late it has become permissible to sport a waistcoat of any conceivable hue, especially at celebratory occasions like weddings. The same is also true of shirts and ties, although if you are not wearing a white shirt, it is best to opt for one that has a colored body teamed with white collar and cuffs. The shirt will have a turn-down collar. What remains firmly beyond the pale is the combination of wing-collared shirt and pre-tied ascot (or cravat) necktie beloved of dress-hire companies, especially when the ascot is teamed with a matching waistcoat.

Shoes will be black and plain Oxford, not patent, which is confined to evening wear, and not brogues. Your accessories are a white or patterned handkerchief in the breast pocket, a floral boutonniere, and, if you wish, gray or lemon gloves—preferably of suede or chamois—and a "white" top hat, which is actually gray in color.

PART TWO

Perfect Grooming

CHAPTER 10

Your Face

Lest you weren't aware, skin is your body's largest organ, covering and protecting everything that lies beneath.

———◆———

Skin is composed of three layers, the lowest one being the subcutaneous layer, which is mostly composed of fat and helps us to keep warm and absorb shocks. It is also where hair production begins. Next comes the dermis containing nerve endings, blood vessels, oil glands, and sweat glands, together with collagen and elastin. Finally, there is the part that we see, the epidermis at the base of which new skin cells form before they rise to the top where they die and are eventually shed, sometimes of their own accord, sometimes aided by processes like shaving. The epidermis is reasonably thick on certain parts of the body, like the soles of your feet and palms of your hands, but becomes thinnest on areas of your face, being just 0.0020 inches deep on the eyelids. You will, therefore, want to give particular care to these places if you want to make sure your skin stays in the best possible condition.

While your face, like your DNA, is unique to you, there are certain characteristics it will share with that of other men. The first of these is that it is different from women's skin. Due to the presence of greater levels of male sex hormones known as androgens, of which testosterone is the best known, a man's skin is about 25 per cent thicker than that of a woman and is thus tougher. It is also firmer, thanks to the presence of greater quantities of collagen and elastin, two naturally occurring proteins. Collagen content is directly related to signs of skin aging, which is why men can sometimes look younger than women of the same age. On the other hand, hitherto most males have been less concerned than their female contemporaries with resisting the visible signs of aging or with using protection against sun damage (of which more later) and so the gender age gap is usually not apparent.

These are the obvious advantages enjoyed by male skin. The principal drawback is that toughness leads to coarseness, with higher levels of testosterone production creating larger pores and more active sebaceous glands. This, in turn, means men are more prone to oiliness, blemishes, and clogged pores, and have a greater inclination to sweat.

Late nights, regular consumption of alcohol (which dehydrates) and nicotine, poor diet, lack of sleep, stress, and sun exposure: these factors all take a toll on your skin and require countermeasures. In fact, one simple but effective—and cheap—way of helping your skin look well is to drink sufficient quantities of water. But you cannot and should not take your skin for granted. Instead, you must treat it with the consideration it deserves.

While the situation has changed of late, traditionally men were disinclined to display much interest in caring for their skin, just as they showed little concern in managing their health. Particularly in relation to the avoidance of conditions like skin cancer, this is not a question of vanity but simple common sense. Nevertheless, getting that message across has been a slow process and there are still plenty of men who believe their masculinity would be called into question if they were discovered applying a sunscreen to their faces.

Taking care of your skin

A regular skin regime is highly recommended, starting with thoroughly cleansing your face twice daily. Although your skin is tougher than that of women, it is still vulnerable to aggressive cleansing. Choose a mild, soap-free cleanser; soap can strip skin of essential oils, leaving it dry and raw. After application, rinse until all the cleanser is removed using warm, but not hot water; the latter is too harsh on the skin. Pat your face dry (don't rub) with a clean towel, preferably not the same one you use after emerging from the bathtub or shower, and make sure your skin is completely free of residual moisture.

Once or twice a week, you might consider exfoliation, which is the removal of old dead cells lying on the skin's outermost surface and has been common practice since the time of the Pharaohs. In any pharmacy, you will be able to find a variety of abrasive products on offer, which usually go by the generic title of skin scrub. As with your cleanser, choose one that contains as few chemicals as possible and is not too aggressive (rubbing a tiny amount between your fingers will let you know if this is going to be the case). You only want to wash away the dead surface skin, not drill down to the subcutaneous layer, so be gentle in application. The benefit is clearer skin, with the likelihood of fewer clogged pores and blemishes.

Although, as a rule, men's skin is oilier than that of women, a number of factors can leave your face, or at least parts of it, feeling dry and sore. This may be caused by air conditioning or central heating, or it may be because of a reaction to shaving; the number of possible explanations is infinite. However, the number of solutions is singular: the application of a decent moisturizer that will help increase the skin's level of hydration. It is now commonly accepted that men should moisturize in order to maintain and even improve their skin's condition. Practically every drugstore, pharmacy, and supermarket has a section dedicated to men's grooming, where you will find a number of inexpensive moisturizers, one of which will suit you. Take a bit of time to ascertain the type of moisturizer that is right for your specific skin, and particularly look out for products that are both light in formula and oil-free: these will be more quickly absorbed and not leave residual shine. And it is best to opt for a brand that's fragrance-free, since some perfumes are inclined to cause irritation to sensitive skin. You can apply moisturizer every morning and night; by doing the latter, you give your skin a clear run of seven or eight hours in which to enjoy the benefits. But if you are using a moisturizer before going to bed, why not apply one without a sun protection factor (SPF)—it's not very likely you are going to suffer from sun damage while asleep.

You may wish to apply a separate cream to the most delicate area around your eyes, one specifically created for this purpose, since a moisturizer intended for the rest of your face will not serve.

Protection from the sun

Many moisturizers make claims about their abilities to counter the visible signs of aging. How much any one product can accomplish in this respect is open to question, and scientists tend to be sceptical about whether topical application can penetrate below the epidermis with real sustained effect. What cannot be disputed are the merits of wearing a moisturizer with a high sun protection factor— at the very minimum factor 15 but preferably closer to 30. While your skin needs a certain amount of Vitamin D to stay healthy, as far as possible you should avoid exposure to direct sun during the key hours of 10am to 3pm.

Of late, skin cancer is the cancer men are most likely to experience:

in 2008, the American Academy of Dermatology reported that of all the people likely to die annually from melanoma (the most lethal form of skin cancer) 64 percent would be men. At the same time, almost 50 percent of the men surveyed announced that they never used a sun screen moisturizer, thereby leaving themselves vulnerable to developing skin cancer. This scenario is changing as awareness campaigns become more effective and ever more families are directly affected by skin cancer. However, men remain at greater risk than women and will continue to be until they all take necessary precautions. An SPF moisturizer should be applied daily and not just during sunny weather; you are at risk from skin damage and cancers like melanoma throughout the year. Certainly, you ought never to expose skin to the sun's rays without first applying ample protection, and then regularly reapplying it.

Getting older
Hair grows where?!

Regardless of how much care you take of yourself and your skin, you will grow older. One sign of this advance in years is the unexpected—and unattractive—appearance of hair in places it never grew before and in quantities you never imagined possible. Suddenly tufts start sprouting from your ears and nostrils, and, as if that wasn't bad enough, your eyebrows grow to resemble bat wings. You must act as soon as you see the first signs of these unhappy developments, which frequently coincide with the permanent departure of hair where you most want to retain it: on top of your head. Keep your eyebrows in check by clipping them with fine scissors every couple of days. Don't pluck your eyebrows: you risk looking like Joan Crawford in one of her hammier roles. Any decent pharmacy will sell you a small electrical device specifically designed to trim the hair in your ears

Don't pluck your eyebrows: you risk looking like Joan Crawford in one of her hammier roles

and nostrils, again something that will require attention several times a week. Don't allow these outbreaks of hirsuteness get out of control; they are one of the most obvious, but also most easily managed, indications of aging.

Blemishes

Unfortunately, male skin has larger pores and is prone to greater oiliness than female skin. As a result, many men suffer from blemishes such as blackheads and acne. One way to minimize the likelihood of these conditions, or to keep them under control, is to follow the skin regime outlined previously on pages 84-86. On the other hand, there are times when greater intervention is required than just regular cleansing and exfoliation.

Acne and other so-called skin blemishes are most prevalent among teenagers whose hormones are especially active. However, this kind of condition is by no means exclusive to puberty and can be more discomforting for adults precisely because it is less common. Beneath the skin surface, a fatty substance called sebum empties into our hair follicles. When it gets stuck, as can sometimes occur, the backup produces what is known as a whitehead: if it is stuck on the surface of the skin and exposed to air, oxygenation will turn it into a blackhead. Once more sebum backs up, pressure grows on the surrounding skin, leaving it red and inflamed. This, simply explained, is acne.

There is nothing "dirty" about blemished skin—the majority of people with acne are, in fact, zealous about cleansing—but Western culture tends to view it as rather unattractive. Because we place a high premium on clear skin, acne is especially unfortunate. It also usually treatable, so there is no need for anyone who has the condition not to find a cure. There are lots of products available in drugstores and pharmacies, and one of these ought to do the job. If not, then it is worth seeing a doctor or dermatologist who will be able to prescribe retinol-based creams and gels designed to produce clear skin. Retinol is a form of Vitamin A, the topical application of which has been shown to clear acne. Don't put up with blemished skin. It can be easily and speedily banished and you will be the beneficiary.

CHAPTER 11

Shaving and Facial Hair

Shaving is an activity that literally separates the men from the boys, and from the opposite sex, too. For most of us, it's a daily activity, one of the rituals of our morning preparation.

———◆———

It has been estimated that the average man will shave 20,000 times during his life, spending around three and a half minutes a day, which adds up to around 900 hours in the 60 years between ages 15 and 75. Given the statistics, you would think that most men will soon learn how to shave properly, but evidence indicates otherwise. Somehow many of us demonstrate that practice doesn't always make perfect: we shave every day, but consistently mess it up.

Luckily, these skills can easily be improved, not least by taking a bit more time and trouble over the task. Rush the job and you are likely to botch it. Schedule just five more minutes than has hitherto been the case for your daily shave and you will experience immediate results—not only an improved appearance but also greater facial comfort because one of the drawbacks to sloppy shaving is physical pain, owing to the increased likelihood of blemishes, nicks, and rawness. Avoid all these hazards by learning how to shave properly. You'll find minimal effort repays with maximum results.

A few useful tips about shaving:

• Consider using a shaving brush made from badger hair. Yes, it adds time to the procedure, but there are advantages: the bristle holds a lot of water, producing a richer lather which in turn ensures less dragging on the skin. Additionally, a brush acts as a gentle exfoliant on your face, removing dead skin cells prior to shaving.

• Whether you opt for a cream or a gel (the latter is often deemed preferable because it helps a blade glide over the skin and is less liable to clog pores), use a product that contains glycerine, since this lubricates and protects. Products containing alcohol, mint or menthol, or other fragrances should be avoided: these can sometimes cause a reaction to skin, which is particularly vulnerable after being shaved.

• Prepare your razor by allowing it to soak for a few seconds in hot water; you'll notice the benefits immediately. Change your blade regularly; every week is recommended. Blades not only become dull with age but also more susceptible to a buildup of residue, which can lead to skin infection.

• If you cut yourself, staunch the bleeding and then apply a styptic pencil (available from drugstores and pharmacies), to stop the blood flowing and also prevent infection.

• After shaving, always apply a balm or moisturizer. This should be unperfumed—the chemicals in some products can cause an allergic reaction on freshly shaven skin—but, ideally, should contain an antiseptic to assist in closing pores and preventing infection.

• Electric razors are preferred by some men, but seemingly some 85 percent of the world's males would sooner experience a wet shave. On the other hand, you ought to own an electric razor: it is invaluable for tidying up any tufts of hair overlooked while wet-shaving or for running over the face on evenings when you have an engagement and want to look your best.

• Anybody with curly hair will know the problem of in-growing hair. One of the best solutions is to soak a face cloth or flannel in hot water and hold this over the afflicted area for a short period. Then use a pair of sterilized tweezers to pluck out the hair causing the problem. Pat the skin dry and apply a little moisturizer.

Facial hair

After puberty, all men have facial hair, albeit of differing density and strength—some men find the bottom half of their faces enveloped in thick dark hair, while others will manage only patchy coverage at best. How much or how little of this you want to leave on display is a matter of choice, although if your hair growth is light, then remaining clean-shaven is probably best: there's something rather inadequate about a wispy beard.

Beards

Beards can be grown for religious reasons (as is the case for Sikhs, who are also forbidden to cut the hair on their heads). In many ancient civilizations, a beard was deemed evidence of strength and virility but it could also serve as a form of decoration. In Egypt under the Pharaohs, for example, the highest caste of men wore hair on their chin, which could be dyed with henna or interwoven with gold thread. And the Pharaohs themselves wore a false metal beard as a sign of sovereignty. However, from the time of Alexander the Great onward, the Greeks and then the Romans preferred to be clean-shaven, regarding beards as evidence of slovenliness: Hadrian was the first Roman Emperor to have worn a beard (seemingly grown to hide facial scars). Early Christians, with their customary habit of going against the popular vote, approved of beards since shaving was

As a rule, women don't like beards. At the same time, other men judged beards made their wearers appear more dignified

indicative of personal vanity, which is why all the first saints and martyrs tend to be shown with luxuriant growth on their chins.

Since then beards have gone in and out of fashion, the last time they were widespread in Europe and the United States being the second half of the 19th century, when full, heavy beards and side-whiskers were hugely popular. Then, in the years after World War I, the clean-shaven face returned to vogue and has remained the preference of the majority ever since. Beards made a reappearance in the 1960s as part of the counter-culture movement, especially among hippies, but they never attained universal support. Such remains the case today: most men shave. On the other hand, daily shaving is tiresome and time-consuming, and for some men also painful. Therefore the alternative option of growing a beard can be appealing. If you do want to go down this route, just bear in mind the following points:

1. It is sometimes suggested that a beard acts as a form of disguise and therefore implies the wearer has something to hide, or is less trustworthy. It is possible that unconsciously all of us assume a bearded man is engaged in some kind of concealment. And there is a widespread urban legend that men with beards are more likely to be stopped at airport security checkpoints because they arouse suspicion.

2. One might also add that, as a rule, women don't like beards (they make a man's face scratchy, apparently). An academic study conducted in New Zealand in 2012 found that women considered men with beards less attractive. At the same time, other men judged beards made their wearers appear more dignified. So, which would you rather have: your dignity or your girl?

3. Beards are prohibited in a number of professions. They are currently not allowed in any branch of the US Military, for example, although some moustaches are still permitted. Sometimes there is a sound reason for the ban: firefighters and airline pilots, for example, need to be clean-shaven to allow for a gas or oxygen mask to fit perfectly to their faces. In other instances, as with members of the armed or police forces in many states, the rule seems dictated primarily by a desire for the workforce to present a uniformly tidy appearance. If you insist on wearing a beard, this may influence your choice of profession.

4. Don't make the mistake of imagining that a beard requires no maintenance. If you are going to have facial hair, then you ought to keep it tidy. This means shaving the lower part of your neck, from around the Adam's apple down, so that it doesn't become populated by straggly hairs, and your beard ends in a clean line instead. And speaking of clean, make sure your beard never acquires evidence of recent food or drink consumption. If we want to know about your last meal, we can ask.

5. You should keep your beard an even length, ideally ensuring it does not grow too long. There are plenty of electrical trimmers, coming with various attachments to keep a beard neat. There's no advantage to keeping the rest of your appearance tidy if your beard then looks a mess.

6. Goatee beards used to be popular among science teachers, who also wore corduroy jackets and knitted wool ties. More recently, the goatee has been discovered by actor Brad Pitt, a handsome man seemingly on a mission to make himself unattractive. There is nothing alluring about the goatee or its sundry variants, like the fulsome Van Dyke

How to Shave Properly

1. Soften the hair on your face, either by splashing it with warm water or by covering it with a warm, damp cloth for a minute or so.

2. If you're susceptible to post-shave rash (and even if not), apply a few drops of pre-shave oil. This will further soften up the skin.

3. Cover the lower section of your face and neck with shaving cream, ideally applied with a badger-hair brush. This will help to build up a rich lather and lift up each whisker.

4. Begin by shaving first one cheek, then the other, down as far as the jaw line and an inch either side of your mouth. Shave with or across— not against—the grain of your beard, as this is the best way to avoid irritation. Shave in short strokes and constantly rinse your blade in clean water.

5. Next shave your neck, again making sure not to run the blade against the beard grain. Finally, tackle around your chin, and below and above your mouth.

6. Once completely shaved, splash with water and then check if any areas have been missed. Once you are clean-shaven, close the pores with plenty of cold water and then pat the skin dry. Finally, but essentially, conclude with the application of a thin layer of moisturizer.

or the close-cut circle beard (otherwise known as a door knocker). And a goatee without an accompanying moustache is the facial equivalent of emerging only half-dressed.

7. There was a fashion in the 1980s, fueled by such icons of the era as singer George Michael and the television series *Miami Vice*, for what became known as "designer stubble" (this, incidentally, was a period when the word designer, hitherto a little-employed noun, turned into an overworked adjective). Designer stubble is neither a beard, nor is it clean-shaven: it is simply evidence that you have too much time on your hands.

8. The same is true of all facial hair that takes a circuitous route about your cheeks and chin. This kind of beard decoration is popular among young men and takes the form of strips of hair trimmed so thin they could be mistaken for lines drawn with a fountain pen. While the workmanship is undoubtedly impressive, one has to conclude: so much effort to so little purpose.

Additional facial hair

Two other items of facial hair also require brief remarks.

Moustaches

It is rare for a man simply to allow the hair between his upper lip and nose to grow unattended. Inevitably, it is subject to grooming, frequently of the most elaborate sort. Some Indian men, for instance, grow enormous handlebar moustaches of the sort favored by the English actor Jimmy Edwards: the world's widest moustache (14 feet long) is worn by Ram Singh Chauhan of India. Related to this is the pencil-thin-but-extended moustache with curled, waxed tips, which was the trademark of Surrealist artist Salvador Dali. In the past, the pencil moustache tended to be the preserve of suave bounders, chaps like Errol Flynn or David Niven, although of late its best-known advocate is alternative filmmaker John Waters. At the opposite extreme is the type of small moustache favoured by, and now forever associated with, Adolf Hitler—and, before him, Charlie Chaplin.

As the above list will indicate, moustaches are often treated by their wearers as an outlet for self-expression and the establishment of a distinctive identity: a heavy burden to place on a minor outbreak of facial hair. But what other purpose can a moustache serve? It is neither one thing nor the other; it has no function except as a piece of decoration and therefore needs to be idiosyncratic. Grow one if you can discover no other means to convey your unique character, but please keep it tidy and clean. And unless you intend to be mistaken for a pornographic actor from the 1970s, do not allow the ends of your moustache to extend below the edge of your mouth.

Sideburns

For the majority of men, their sideburns take the shape of neat rectangles extending no lower than the earlobe. This is an orderly way to keep a sideburn, signaling the right degree of virility held in check. *Autres temps, autres mœurs:* during the Napoleonic era, and particularly among members of the military, luxurious side whiskers

The moustache has no function except as a piece of decoration and therefore needs to be idiosyncratic

became the norm. These, in turn, developed into the vast bushy beards widely worn throughout the Victorian era. But when the beards went at the start of the last century, so, too, did the sideburns. They were brought back in the late 1950s and early 1960s as a sign of youthful rebellion, although those developed by Elvis Presley have since acquired a significance that is more ironic than iconic. Depending on your degree of hirsuteness, sideburns, like moustaches, can take whatever form you choose to give them. But the more elaborate that form, the greater amount of attention it will demand. Ultimately, the simplest solution is to keep sideburns short and tidy. You have more constructive ways to pass the day than fiddling with the hair on your cheeks.

CHAPTER 12

Hair

It was St. Paul, always a reliable source for quotations, who first proclaimed hair a crowning glory. In this instance, he was specifically referring to women, which just goes to prove that Biblical quotes are not necessarily reliable: in the Old Testament's Song of Solomon, for example, the narrator at one point proclaims, "Thy hair is as a flock of goats that appear from Mount Gilead." Most of us have seen men with that kind of bushy hair and it's never an attractive spectacle.

———◆———

Regardless of St. Paul's gender bias, there's no reason why a man's hair should be, if not a crowning glory, then certainly a definite asset. After all, it is likely to be one of the first things people you meet will notice and, whether you like the idea or not, they are liable to judge you by the state of your hair. If it's dirty and/or messy, unfavorable conclusions will be drawn about your character. One way to make a good first impression, therefore, is to keep your hair clean and tidy. That way nobody will have an erroneous opinion of you.

The barber

Like so much else about your appearance, hair should look terrific without indicating anything much has been done to achieve its present superlative condition. Here you have the opportunity to practice the art that conceals art, giving the impression of natural spontaneity despite the time and effort required to achieve this. But even if you're not going to make a lot of effort or spend much time on your hair, abide by the rules of perpetual cleanliness and tidiness, and you'll be fine.

So, above all, make sure you schedule a regular haircut, ideally every month, even if this only entails the ends being trimmed. Why not make a point of having your hair cut on the first Monday or last Saturday or whatever? That way, you will find it easy to remember when it is time to visit the barber.

As for the latter, finding the right barber is like finding the right barman; you might be lucky and get it right first time, or you might have to trawl a lot of joints before coming across the place where you feel at home. Your barber should be not just competent at his job (in the sense that he doesn't send you home with a head full of nicks), but also understand what style works best for you. In addition, he needs to have some understanding of the human character and appreciate your temperament. This is the trait that barbers share with barmen: the best ones are empathetic and can offer advice whenever it is required. Just as many women like to confide in their hairdresser, so a lot of men like to have personal conversations with their barber, even if it is only to exchange an opinion on the weekend sports results. Any decent barber becomes an amateur therapist as he cuts and shaves, providing customers with an opportunity to discuss whatever topics they wish. On the other hand, if you prefer to have your hair cut in silence, the barber should understand that as well; it helps to bring a newspaper or book when you sit down. Alternatively, keep your eyes closed, although this means you can't see what the barber is doing to your hair.

Once you have established a good relationship with your barber—make sure you tip him at the end of every visit—you can feel free to drop by after a fortnight or so just to have the back of your neck and the area around your ears given a quick trim. It will help to keep your hair neat and means you'll only need to have a full cut once each month. Tidying these areas is a task that takes no more than five minutes but makes all the difference.

One other point: your own high standards of cleanliness should be shared by your barber. Watch that he sterilizes all his equipment and uses a fresh blade when shaving the back of your neck. Otherwise you risk catching an infection passed on from another customer. The barber's premises should also be well maintained, with all hair swept up from the floor after every cut.

Choosing the right style

Like your clothes, you should wear your hair in the style that best suits your features. It is worth taking a little trouble to find out what works for your facial shape and coloring, and then keeping to the same style. Not all men look good with very short hair, while few of us can carry off long hair, certainly after the age of 30. There is usually a happy medium that will be right for you. Don't be afraid to experiment; one of the great advantages of hair is that it grows back (at the rate of about half an inch per month), so if you make a mistake, it will naturally correct itself within a relatively short space of time. Settle on a style and length that works best with your face and shows it off to advantage. This is one of the reasons adolescent boys are inclined to grow their hair long: it hides features to which they are still becoming accustomed. By adulthood, you ought to have worked out what are your best facial attributes, and decided on a hairstyle that complements them. Consider changing your hair as you grow older. The wild style you wore as a youth probably doesn't look so good now that your hair has turned gray. It is possible your choice of hair length and style will be governed by your career. Many jobs require employees to keep their hair short and neat. Sometimes, as with the military and police force, this is an official ruling. More often it is an informal but universally understood directive, especially in professions like banking or law. As with so much else about our appearance, there is no logic behind this, simply awareness that we are all judged, consciously or unconsciously, on the basis of how we look. Short, tidy hair is deemed to indicate reliability whereas, for the past century, long hair has been considered evidence of a rebellious temperament (not a quality prized in the military or in financial services), and therefore unacceptable. For this reason, longer hair tends to be found mainly among men working in more creative professions, such as advertising or broadcasting.

Taking care of your hair
Washing

Cleanliness is as important as tidiness. You need to wash your hair regularly, but just how often depends on a number of factors: how greasy it becomes over successive days, for example, and in what sort of environment you work and live. Another factor to be taken into account is the buildup of styling products in your hair, which have to be cleaned out after a few days. Nevertheless, bear in mind that too much washing is harmful, since it strips the scalp of naturally defensive oils and does not allow time for them to be replenished. Even if you only wash your hair twice a week, do so with a gentle shampoo and conditioner. Avoid any products with too many chemicals and perfumes, as these could cause an allergic reaction.

Dandruff

A common phenomenon among men is dandruff; seemingly, it affects half the post-pubertal population. Dandruff is residual evidence of the scalp shedding dead skin cells. In itself dandruff is not dirty or harmful, but it looks unattractive to have a blanket of white flakes on your shoulders and can be the cause of embarrassment. Most cases can be treated and resolved by using one of the anti-dandruff shampoos widely available. Again, be aware that some of the contents in your shampoo and conditioner, or in your styling products, may be exacerbating an inclination toward dandruff. Sometimes just changing one of these items results in a return to dandruff-free hair. If the problem is more extreme and defies home treatment, it will be necessary to see a dermatologist who will be able to prescribe an appropriate solution, such as the topical application of corticosteroids that combat skin conditions.

Styling products

After washing and drying your hair, you will most probably want to finish with one or more styling products. Until the 1980s, there used to be only one such item available to men, Brylcreem, a pomade invented in 1928 which left evidence of its presence in your hair on shirt collars, sheets and pillow cases, and any other fabric it touched. More recently, other options have become available and today, as even the most cursory glance over supermarket shelves will testify, there is a daunting range of styling products on offer.

Once more, the only way to discover what works best for your hair is engaging in a process of trial and error. Aside from gels, there are many mousses, pastes, creams, and serums, the work of any or all of

It is essential you don't betray the fact that time and effort went into your hair grooming

which can be finished off with a spritz or more of hairspray. The purpose of these products is to help your hair stay neat through the course of a day. Accordingly, the perfect scenario should be that your hair remains in place but is not so locked into position that anyone wishing to run a hand through it encounters an impenetrable helmet. The popularity among the young for gravity-defying hairstyles, in particular great tufts of hair that shoot skyward from the forehead, should be the cause of amusement not emulation. This style is achieved only by the deployment of industrial quantities of hair gel and spray, and is so brittle it could probably be snapped off. Rest assured: any man who at present wears his hair in this way will, in a few years' time, be paying serious money to ensure all photographic evidence of his tonsorial misdemeanor is destroyed. Again, it is essential you don't betray the fact that time and effort went into your hair grooming; those locks must look as though they artfully arranged themselves on your scalp. Never overload your hair with styling product because, once again, this could cause an adverse reaction. In addition, too much product is harder to remove when you wash your hair, so apply the minimum necessary.

To dye or not to dye?

Should men color their hair? Not so many years ago, nobody would have thought to ask such a question; just as men never used anything in their hair except a dab of Brylcreem, so they lived and died with whatever color their hair was at the time (as opposed to living and dying). Personal intervention in the matter was absolutely inconceivable. Not so today, when many men do color their hair, either choosing to visit a hairdresser for a professional application, or doing the job themselves with one of the kits available in many supermarkets, drugstores, and pharmacies.

Professional work on your hair will usually take the form of highlights and lowlights, that is, applying a hair colorant to strands of your hair. This can be done with the use of foil, with a brush, or by methods known as "frosting" and "clunking," which broadly involve a more free-hand approach to using dye. There is also the process of bleaching, which effectively strips the natural color from your hair. Home kits tend to feature a brush, although they can also allow for the application of a single color to your whole head. Incidentally, other than price there appears to be no real difference between the kits sold to men and those targeted at women (the former usually prove to be more expensive).

Ultimately, it is a matter of personal choice but once you engage in hair coloring it becomes difficult to stop. Like Botox or cosmetic surgery, dyeing hair requires ongoing—and potentially costly—maintenance, otherwise after a couple of weeks its presence will be apparent as your natural hair color begins to appear at the roots. Young men tend to dye their hair because it is fashionable. Older men, on the other hand, most often do so because they want to hide evidence that they are going gray. It is true that gray hair can make you appear older than you might wish, but so can many other things, such as drab skin or lack of animation in your features. In a competitive job market, youthfulness, with its accompanying attributes of energy and enthusiasm, is at a premium. So it is understandable that signs of aging can be unwelcome. Nevertheless, ultimately you will find engaging with hair dye a self-defeating process: there are few more visible signs of creeping age than hair that is unnaturally rich in color above a lined face. Better to leave

A brief guide to what hair style works best with each facial shape:

- **Oval Face:** Generally considered the ideal, since it is most balanced, and almost any hair style will suit. But other features, like your nose, might be more prominent than average, so take this into account when making your decision.

- **Long Face:** You want to diminish length, so opt for a hair style that is longer and fuller on the sides and relatively short on top, as this will help to provide balance.

- **Triangular Face:** Is wider at the forehead than the chin and often has prominent cheekbones. A long fringe or bangs, perhaps with a side parting, will help to even the impression (and a beard is also advantageous in filling out the lower section of the face).

• **Round Face:** You will want to lengthen your features, so no full or wide hair styles. Instead, go for the reverse of what is prescribed for men with long faces, i.e. keep the hair short at the sides and fuller on top.

• **Square Face:** Not dissimilar from the round face, but with a more defined jawline and sometimes skull. In this instance, still keep hair short at the sides and with a soft fullness on top of the head.

• **Diamond Face:** Widest in the middle around the cheekbones. To play down this feature, wear your hair longer at the sides and have a full fringe or bangs on top.

your hair its natural color, even if this is gray or white, and find other means of projecting youthful dynamism.

Losing your hair

And so to baldness, which again can be the cause of much angst. Hair loss usually begins on either side of the forehead, with the resultant receding hairline, and on the crown of the head. Eventually the two meet and you are undeniably and inescapably bald. Genetic inheritance is the most common reason for losing your hair: if other males in your family, either maternal or paternal, went bald, you're also likely to do so. Seemingly, DHT, a form of testosterone, is responsible for inducing baldness, so all those stories about bald men being more virile have at least some basis in truth. On the other hand, just to complicate matters, one of the main reasons why older men lose their hair is because there is a decrease in the amount of testosterone the body will produce. Whatever the explanation, the fact remains that if you're genetically predisposed to baldness, it will more than likely happen.

There are a number of responses you can have to this condition. One is denial, which usually involves growing whatever hair you still have and then tortuously wrapping or scraping it across your scalp to give the (not very convincing) impression that you still luxuriate in tonsorial splendor. You will dread strong winds lest they disturb your artwork and reveal the baldness beneath. For the same reason, you will also live in fear of anyone touching your hair.

Secondly, you can seek out treatment to restore or replace your missing hair. There are a huge number of options available today, ranging from oral applications to operations. Some are more successful than others; all are likely to cost you a lot of money. If, however, your baldness is costing you even more angst, then finding a means to give you back a full head of hair will be deemed a price worth paying. As with gray hair, it seems men worry that baldness makes them look prematurely old and therefore less attractive or dynamic. But, again like gray hair, there are many ways to project a zestful personality other than the presentation of a fully follicled scalp.

Another possibility is that you wear a wig. This used to be a more widespread recourse than is now the case. You can choose from wigs made of human hair, horsehair, or various synthetic materials. Realistically, you shouldn't consider any of them. Of all the options open to you, a wig is the least attractive.

Finally, you can accept that you're going or have gone bald, and not give the matter any further thought. This is without doubt the best course of action and the one that will cost you least, either in worry or money. If you are losing your hair, cut what remains short. Your barber can run a trimmer over your scalp and ensure an even appearance. There are also electrical devices you can buy to perform the same task at home. As with so much else about your appearance, the most important point is that you look clean and tidy.

CHAPTER 13

Teeth

A good smile ought to be among your most engaging features; it will certainly be one of the features that people notice first about you. However, the impression you make will not be positive if you have poor teeth (or if, owing to the bad state of your teeth, you keep your mouth permanently clamped shut).

———◆———

Taking good care of your teeth

So how should you be brushing? Well, first of all the process should take at least two minutes and cover back as well as front teeth. Make sure you don't miss out on any areas. Start with the outer surfaces, working from the back forward. Try to spend some time on the inside of your teeth before finishing, paying extra attention to the biting surfaces. Always brush from gum to tooth and do not use a jerking vertical motion, as this can lead to gum recession and the exposure of parts of your teeth not protected by enamel.

Toothpaste

In this task, you are likely to use toothpaste. Like toothbrushes, this has a long and sometimes equally unattractive history (soot and salt have already been mentioned). The main function of tooth cleaning materials in the past was to provide an element of abrasion in order to remove traces of food. So the ancient Greeks and Romans used crushed bones or oyster shells, which sound only marginally more appealing than coal dust. Until the end of the 19th century, tooth powders were the norm, rather than pastes, and they could be made from a diverse range of ingredients, to which water would be added. Pastes were gradually introduced from the 1890s onward, with various flavors added to make them more palatable (and to give the user that "fresh breath" experience). Fluoride, which can help to prevent dental decay, was introduced around the same time as pastes made their debut, but only became widespread from the 1950s onward.

Modern toothpastes perform much the same function as their ancient equivalents, albeit in a more attractive fashion. Mostly they provide abrasion, together with a pleasant aftertaste. Any additional claims should be regarded with a degree of skepticism. The ability of toothpastes to clean, and to whiten, is limited: the most important aspect to looking after your teeth lies in good brushing technique, not in the ingredients of your paste. A small but important point: change your toothbrush regularly, at least once every three months.

The impression you make on prospective partners will not be positive if you have poor teeth

Otherwise the bristles become too worn and can no longer do their job effectively. And rinse the brush head in very hot water after every use, to minimize the risk of germs collecting and causing infection in your mouth.

Flossing

Don't imagine that once you have finished brushing your teeth, all maintenance work is done. Next you should floss. Dental floss is made from a series of micro-fine filaments, which are gently inserted between two teeth and then scraped along their respective surfaces in order to remove any residue of food or plaque. A New Orleans dentist called Levi Spear Parmly apparently proposed floss, made from silk fibers, in 1815 but the call was largely ignored; only at the very end of the 19th century did Johnson & Johnson take out the first commercial patent for dental floss. Take-up remained poor, however, until around the time of World War II, when nylon floss was invented and proved to be better than silk, having greater abrasion resistance and elasticity.

Despite the widely appreciated benefits of flossing, many people continue only to brush their teeth. For the sake of your dental hygiene, you should do both, and should learn how to floss properly. Wind a piece of the filament approximately 18 inches long between the middle fingers of your two hands. Next, gently but firmly slide a piece of floss up and down between each pair

If you want to make a good impression, you should start looking after the contents of your mouth

of teeth, making sure you reach under the gum line. Move the floss along between your fingers so that you are not using the same strip between all teeth. If you are not used to flossing, you may find your gums bleed—don't let this put you off. Bleeding is just a temporary reaction and your gums will grow healthier and stronger thanks to a regular flossing routine.

The interdental brush

Follow with a third piece of equipment: the interdental brush. This is a small device with disposable heads fitted onto a plastic handle that is deployed to remove any remaining bits of food trapped between teeth. It is also invaluable for cleaning between the wire of dental braces, if you are wearing these. Interdental brushes come in a variety of sizes and you will need to find which one is right for you, depending on the width of gaps between teeth. As with toothbrushes, change your interdental brush on a routine basis.

Mouthwash

And now, it is time to conclude with a rinse of mouthwash, although preferably with something better tasting than what was proposed by Hippocrates: the ancient Greek physician recommended an interesting mixture of salt, aluminum sulfate, and vinegar. Regardless of any claims made on the container in relation to whitening or bacteria-killing, do not expect too much from your mouthwash. It is not a substitute for any of the previous activities but complements and concludes them, leaving you with a clean mouth and fresh breath. Many dentists recommend using a mouthwash low in, or free of, alcohol.

The dentist

Speaking of dentists, you ought to schedule an appointment every six months or so, in order to have your teeth checked. If you have been taking good care of them and following the twice-daily regime outlined above, the dentist will have little to do other than congratulate you on your admirable oral hygiene. But there may be problems lurking beneath the surface that only a dentist can detect (taking x-rays is now a standard procedure) and, as in all other areas of medicine, prevention is superior to cure, as well as usually being the cheaper option.

In any case, your visit will also provide an opportunity to have your teeth examined by a dental hygienist who can assess your current regime and perhaps encourage better practice: it is surprising how many of us don't even brush our teeth properly, let alone follow through with adequate flossing and interdental cleaning. Learning good oral health is invaluable because it will lead to less work being performed on your teeth (with consequent cost savings).

The other advantage to scheduling regular dental surgery visits is that they should include a professional cleaning of your teeth. Bear in mind that some food and drink is likely to discolor teeth. Villains include tea, coffee, and red wine; the more you consume of these, the more likely there is to be evidence of their intake on your teeth. Cigarette smoking is also harmful to your teeth: nicotine not only builds up stains but also inflicts damage on the enamel and gums. Even with the most rigorous efforts on your part, it is probable that tartar, which is mineralized plaque, will have built up in those parts of your mouth that are hardest to reach with a toothbrush and dental floss. Professional cleaning ensures this is cleared away, that your teeth are given a good polish, and all evidence of what you have been consuming in recent months is removed.

Whiter than white

Do you want, or need, to go further? There are a number of procedures offered by dentists that will improve, or even fundamentally alter, the appearance of your teeth. The most common of these is whitening. It is a fact that as we age, the mineral content of our teeth changes due to enamel becoming less porous and more mineral-deficient. In other words, yellow teeth in the elderly are not necessarily a sign of dental decay. But since white teeth are highly prized, all of us would prefer to keep the contents of our mouth that color.

You can now buy teeth-whitening kits for use at home. These work by the application of a bleaching agent, usually placed in a plastic tray, which is then fitted onto the upper and lower jaw for a short period. There are also mouthguards and dental strips that perform the same function, although the latter will contain a lower concentration of bleaching agent and therefore produce weaker results. The effectiveness of these whiteners varies widely from one individual to the next. In addition, each jurisdiction's health authority tends to permit different levels of bleaching agent; in some countries, it is very low and likely to have a negligible impact on the color of your teeth.

There are obvious advantages to having your teeth whitened by a professional, not least the assurance that the procedure will yield visible results. Furthermore, before any whitening takes place, your teeth ought to be scrupulously examined in advance to make sure the process will not lead to any side-effects. A good dentist will curb your wish to have excessively white teeth. Naturally, if you are spending money on whitening, which is never cheap, you will want the best possible outcome. But bear in mind that teeth that appear too white, like teeth that are uniformly even, will not look natural,

*Learning good oral health is invaluable
and will lead to less work being performed
on your teeth*

especially if you are no longer in the first flush of youth. The most efficacious intervention should be the least apparent. Far from improving your appearance in an undetectable fashion, dazzling white teeth will clearly proclaim that work has been done on your mouth. Resist the temptation to go for snow-white teeth and settle on a lighter shade than is presently the case but still one that is credible for a man of your age.

The same rule applies to any other dental procedure you undertake: there should be no evidence it ever occurred. Sometimes work is essential—such as having a crown or an implant—sometimes optional, like having old metal fillings replaced with white ones. More adults today than used to be the case consider having their teeth straightened, which involves wearing braces for several months or even longer. There are various kinds of braces, including a clear variety for anyone who feels self-conscious about the process. You could be wearing braces for cosmetic reasons or because your dentist feels it necessary to correct a problem like a defective under- or overbite. Whatever the reason, make sure the outcome leaves the contents of your mouth looking better than they did before, but not looking unnaturally flawless. It is the small imperfections in our features, such as a gap between two front teeth, which render us distinctive from everyone else. Homogeneity, even in matters dental, is not to be encouraged.

CHAPTER 14

Body, Hands, and Feet

John Wesley, the 18th-century founder of Methodism, once famously declared that cleanliness is indeed next to godliness.

❖

Consequently, your chances of becoming a living deity will be immeasurably improved if you are able to maintain a continual state of cleanliness. Failure to do so will not only diminish your godlike status but also find you shunned by the majority of the population—particularly by members of the opposite sex or anyone in close proximity to you—as an accumulation of body odor renders your company steadily more offensive. Just as our clothes need to be washed regularly to keep them clean, so, too, do our bodies.

Body

Failure to wash leads to poor hygiene, which, in turn, renders us more vulnerable to disease and infection. One of the most important ways in which Florence Nightingale improved standards of nursing in Victorian Britain was to insist on basic hygiene in hospitals. As a result, levels of infection and mortality among patients dropped.

Bodily cleanliness is regularly equated with moral purity: clean people are deemed to be good people. The Christian faith, for

In a world where water is an increasingly precious and costly resource, showers are the best way to wash

example, proposes the notion that sins are washed away in the sacrament of baptism, which is a form of ritual cleansing. Likewise, Muslims consider it important that believers should be clean in body and spirit alike, with Mohammed declaring, "A Muslim is required to be pure morally and spiritually as well as physically." This link between cleanliness and goodness means dirt is often proclaimed as "bad," although it has no inherent behavioral characteristics. All of which helps to explain why Wesley ascribed godliness to the clean.

"Cleanliness," wrote the 19th-century cultural historian Jacob Burckhardt, "is indispensable to our modern notion of social perfection." When he made this statement over 150 years ago, general standards of cleanliness and opportunities to become and remain clean were far less widespread than is the case today. Improvements in plumbing since 1900 mean we are much cleaner than our ancestors, for whom bathing was an infrequent activity, performed perhaps once a week at most. While the ancient Romans had large public baths that were open to, and frequented by, all citizens, thereafter access to such facilities greatly declined, with a corresponding drop in standards of cleanliness. Even the act of assembling and heating sufficient water for a bath meant few people troubled to wash themselves much. As a result, the past was not only another country, to quote L.P. Hartley's dictum, but also a much smellier one.

There is no longer any reason for you to remain unwashed unless you are making some kind of personal protest against the act of bathing, or decline to clean yourself on obscure ethical grounds.

Although too much washing can lead to dry and rough skin—water strips our bodies of their natural oils—we ought to bathe once a day. Whether you take a bath or shower is a matter of personal choice, but it should be pointed out that baths use up more water and are therefore more expensive, as well as time-consuming. There is also an argument to be made that when you sit in a bath, you are effectively wallowing in your own dirt. While an occasional bath can be recommended, especially as a means of relieving sore muscles after extreme exertion or to ease tension at the end of a stressful day, this should probably not be your customary means of washing.

In a world where water is an increasingly precious and costly resource, showers are the best way to wash. They are fast and economical, and do the job just as well as—if not better than—a bath. When in the shower, the most important body parts to be cleansed on a daily basis are your armpits and groin area, both of which hold large concentrations of the apocrine sweat glands that first become active during puberty. We need to sweat or, to use the more genteel term, perspire, because this is our body's form of thermoregulation. As we become too warm, our skin yields moisture, the evaporation of which has a cooling effect. So we sweat in order to cool down. On average, men perspire more quickly than women and produce greater quantities of sweat, particularly when engaged in exercise.

Dealing with excess perspiration

Some men sweat more than others, and if you are a heavy sweater, this can be embarrassing, especially in today's Western culture where it is deemed ideal to remain perspiration-free at all times: keeping your cool means remaining devoid of sweat. At his party conference in 2000, Britain's then-Prime Minister Tony Blair was photographed delivering a speech in a blue shirt drenched in sweat, and while efforts were made to proclaim this a sign of his passion, it is notable that politicians ever since have studiously avoided wearing colored shirts at key moments in their careers. So opposed is our society to visible evidence of perspiration that, of late, there has been a fashion for underarm Botox injections: just as the toxin can freeze the muscles on your forehead and stop you frowning, so it paralyzes the nerve endings of sweat glands.

There is a condition called hyperhidrosis, otherwise known as excessive sweating. All of us have suffered from this at some time or another, usually when we find ourselves in the middle of a heatwave or a situation that leaves us feeling uncomfortable. But for some men this is a serious issue caused by over-active sweat glands and can be treated either by medication or, in certain circumstances, by surgery (which results in removal of the glands).

Obviously there is nothing inherently dirty about sweat: it is simply a mechanical process that we share with many other mammals. While perspiration is composed primarily of water, it also contains small quantities of minerals, lactic acid, and urea. If this combination of elements remains on our skin for too long, particularly in zones like the underarm area where little light or air penetrates, they will start to ferment and produce what can, over time, become an unpleasant smell. This is why we need to wash ourselves, in anticipation of developing body odor, more usually known as BO. Wash the regions where this is most prevalent with a soap-free cleanser and afterward rinse thoroughly.

As for the rest of your body, unless particular areas are especially dirty, you need be less scrupulous. Bear in mind that we all have a unique scent, one that is detectable to everyone both physically and emotionally close to us. You don't want to lose one of the traits specific to you by over-assiduous scrubbing or, indeed, the excessive use of perfume (of which more later); that would be like destroying part of your DNA.

After drying yourself thoroughly with a clean towel, you will most likely want to apply a deodorant or antiperspirant. It's worth pointing out the differences between the two products since they are often considered to perform the same task. Deodorants do not interfere with the production of sweat but prevent the development of odor through the presence of antiseptic agents, and very often by the addition of a fragrance. The first commercial deodorant was invented around the end of the 19th century and marketed as Mum. Antiperspirants, on the other hand, only became available in the 1940s. Unlike deodorants, these products contain chemical compounds that are designed to block your pores to inhibit the discharge of sweat. As a rule, they are also scented. Antiperspirants contain aluminum compounds as an active ingredient to stop sweat forming. A small number of people will be allergic to this ingredient and develop a skin rash but for most of us there are no side effects. You could find yourself suffering from skin burn due to excessive use of antiperspirant, so don't overdo it: sweating is a natural process intended to lower your body temperature and ought to be permitted, especially if you wash yourself often.

Should you sweat a lot, don't overlook the merits of talcum powder, a natural mineral composed of magnesium silicate. Today it is mostly used on babies to prevent the development of nappy rash, but the powder's absorbent qualities make it a useful ally in countering evidence of perspiration. After you have washed and dried yourself, rub some talc over your body and you'll find it helps to keep you dry over the coming hours.

Your hands

Hands are one of the most hardworking parts of our body, yet we are inclined to take them for granted and show little appreciation of their sterling efforts. They are also one of the first things, along with good teeth and clear eyes, that other people will notice about us. For this reason it is important that we put the best hand forward whenever in company, yet it is astonishing how many men fail to do so. Instead, they frequently present a pair of paws that are calloused and covered in cuts, with ragged, untidy nails, each loaded with a generous quantity of dirt.

No doubt, a lot of men mistakenly hold the opinion that paying attention to their hands is effeminate and/or a waste of their valuable time and money. Especially if they're employed in farming or construction work, their hands are likely to be subjected to a lot of abuse and, they would probably argue, the last thing they need to do is pamper their mitts with various lotions, creams, and treatments. Well, perhaps they should think a little less about themselves and a little more about the rest of us, particularly their partners and families, who have to put up with their hoary hands on a regular basis.

They might also like to take into account that a small amount of care could have the effect of ensuring they do an even better job than is now the case: coarse and rough hands lose their sensitivity, making them less capable than those that have been well maintained of performing tasks that require a certain level of dexterity. In any case, and especially in contemporary urban environments, the majority of men are not professionally engaged in activities that demand their hands are submitted to regular misuse. Since when was tapping a computer keyboard or clicking the button on a mouse so physically demanding on our hands? Ought holding a cell phone and sending a text message be deemed manual labor? Under these circumstances, failure to look after your hands can be regarded as due to nothing better than foolish indifference and laziness.

Basic hand care

The first, and most obvious, task is to keep your hands clean. This means washing them regularly (and, one might add here, especially after visiting the lavatory; it is truly astonishing how many men seem to believe they needn't engage in this elementary act of social courtesy). There is a much wider appreciation today than was formerly the case of how infectious bacilli and viral infections are spread through unwashed hands. In recent years, the importance of clean hands has become particularly important in hospitals, where various potentially life-threatening illnesses can be caught simply because someone in the building did not engage in this basic act. So even if you're not a doctor or nurse, you have an obligation to the rest of us to wash your hands thoroughly and regularly.

Rough and calloused hands are not pleasant either to look at or to feel. They will let you down, particularly if you have taken trouble over the rest of your appearance. Keep the skin on your hands soft by investing in a tube of hand cream and apply it every day. If, during the winter, you suffer from chilblains, a condition caused by cold and humidity, and leading to redness, itching, and cracked skin, make sure to apply strong hand cream to counter the complaint.

Dirty, unkempt nails will reflect badly on you and cannot be

Failure to look after your hands can be regarded as due to nothing better than foolish indifference and laziness

*Nail-biting is a childish habit for which
there is no excuse in adulthood*

tolerated. If you watch black and white films from the 1930s and 1940s, you will frequently see the protagonist receiving a professional manicure. This procedure has now fallen from favor among men but it is perfectly possible for you to perform the same job in your own home. An undemanding and simple procedure, it takes just a few minutes and can be done while you're sitting in front of the television. Begin by keeping the surface beneath your nails clean, using a brush designed for this purpose while you are taking a bath or shower. The shaped end of a nail file will allow you to remove any excess dirt. Gently nudge it between nail and skin without pushing too hard against the latter.

Using either scissors or clippers, trim your nails at least once a week so that they are never more than about one-eighth of an inch in length. Tidy off each nail edge by running an emery board along the top to leave a consistent smooth curve. Nail-biting is a childish habit for which there is no excuse in adulthood. Not only will it make you look puerile but your hands will also look a mess.

Your feet

At least during the winter months, your feet will most likely not be as visible as your hands, but that doesn't mean they're undeserving of the same care. In fact, since more men wear sandals for more of the time each year, it becomes imperative that they take care of their feet, if only to spare the rest of us the sight of their hoary gnarled toes and heels. Should you be one of those individuals who believe flip-flops represent the future of footwear, then give a thought for everyone else and put only your best foot forward.

Establishing a routine

You will find that a once-weekly foot care regime will help to minimize odor and avoid the build up of cracked or scaly skin and calluses. Take time one evening out of seven to soak your feet in warm water into which a little cider vinegar has been added. After a couple of minutes of soaking remove all areas of callusing, especially on the heel and around the top of your toes with a pumice stone, which can be bought in any decent pharmacy. Next, cut and tidy up your toenails. After drying your feet, apply a moisturizing cream similar to that used on your hands; this will minimize the build-up of calluses over the next week.

Keeping your feet in good condition will help to minimize the likelihood of unpleasant smells. Foot odor derives from the build-up of sweat because this is one of those parts of our anatomy prone to moisture outbreaks. As with sweat elsewhere, the condition isn't inherently smelly but becomes so if left untreated. This is especially the case if you wear the same shoes every day and don't allow them to rest between use. Socks made from artificial fibers like polyester and nylon generally also provide less ventilation and may encourage more perspiration than those manufactured from cotton or wool. Only buy the latter and change them, along with your shoes, on a daily basis. If you suffer from a severe dose of foot odor, it can be rectified by the deployment of sodium bicarbonate, an ingredient that is also used in baking. Rub a few pinches of this onto the soles of your feet every day, and put a few inside your shoes as well, and you will find the bad smells soon disappear. Keep your feet in top condition and you will be the principal beneficiary.

CHAPTER 15

Bodily Adornment

Early human societies were much given to bodily adornment, most likely owing to a shortage of good tailors. Unable to order a decent suit, one sufficiently well-cut to disguise his thickening waistline and sloping shoulders, primitive man resorted to other distractions, such as a bone belonging to a deceased enemy worn through his septum. Thankfully, over the intervening millennia we have grown more sophisticated in our presentation, and less inclined to wear parts of our opponents.

———•———

Tattoos

The practice of tattooing dates back to the Neolithic period. The word, however, is a relatively recent addition to the English language, courtesy of the naturalist and botanist Sir Joseph Banks, who accompanied Captain James Cook on his voyage around the world on board HMS *Endeavour* (1768–1771). In his journal for August 1769, Banks, who was then in Tahiti, wrote in his logbook of the indigenous population: "I shall now mention their method of painting their bodies, or 'tattow,' as it is called in their language. This they do by inlaying the color black under their skins in such a manner as to be indelible; everyone is marked thus in different parts of his body accordingly maybe to his humor or different circumstances of his life."

Tattooing is a more ancient and widespread form of body adornment than was then realized by Banks. In 1991, the body of a man who had died some 5,200 years ago was discovered on the Austro-Italian border in the Alps. On his body were some 58 tattoos—simple dots and little crosses distributed in a seemingly random manner. However, further investigation suggested that the tattoos' location—on the lower spine and at knee and ankle joints—indicated they were applied in the hope of alleviating pain, likely caused by arthritis, and accordingly intended to be therapeutic rather than a mark of social status.

On the other hand, the latter function has often been the reason for the application of tattoos. In pre-Christian Britain, for example, tattooing among tribal leaders was widespread. In fact, one tribe living in eastern and northern Scotland, the Picts, are so named because the Romans knew them as "Picti," that is, "painted people."

The Romans themselves did not engage in tattooing, except for criminals and slaves, in other words as a means of demonstrating the lowest status: a legal inscription found in Ephesus indicates that slaves exported to Asia were tattooed with the words "tax paid." Soldiers and gladiators also took to having their faces tattooed but this practice was banned in the 4th century by the Emperor Constantine after he converted to Christianity, since he believed it disfigured "that made in God's image."

It is astonishing to see how, more than 1,700 years after this imperial prohibition, tattooing has returned to widespread fashion. Various arguments have been made to present the practice as perfectly acceptable, not least on the basis of historical precedent.

Unless you plan to flash your Mensa membership card alongside your tattoos, you can expect 25 percent of people you encounter to assume you are dim

However, do not presume that antiquity ensures respectability (note that in ancient times it was mostly slaves or soldiers who were tattooed), or that just because certain people in positions of authority once wore tattoos you are now justified in doing so. For example, it is often noted that George V had a dragon tattooed on one of his arms in 1882 while in Japan, and Queen Victoria was rumored to have a small tattoo on her person. That was then, this is now. Besides, since when did the British royal family start acting as the measure for correct behavior? Henry VIII had six wives, two of whom he executed: would you cite him as a role model in any discussion on marriage? It is also worth pointing out that at the time he acquired the aforementioned tattoo, George V was a teenager serving in the Royal Navy and not expected to become King (his older brother was then still alive). The combination of these circumstances and, in particular, the fact that he was an adolescent and really ought to have asked his parents' permission first, absolves him from responsibility for his actions. And unless you are likewise a royal teen visiting the Far East, it also absolves you from any obligation to imitate George V's behavior. The other role model in this area is David Beckham. Again, unless you are a multimillionaire soccer player with an underwear-advertising contract and your own range of sportswear, there is no need for you to have one or several tattoos.

Tattoos frequently seem to be acquired when the wearer is drunk and/or under the influence of other substances. This information is based on one viewing of *The Hangover Part II* while on a long-haul flight, but that does not necessarily invalidate its merit. After all, if, like the unfortunate character in that film, you had a chance to evaluate the advantages of acquiring a tattoo in the chill light of day, it is probable you would decide against doing so, not least because of societal judgment. A survey carried out in the United States in January 2012 found that while one in five adults now has a tattoo, two in five of the people questioned thought tattoo wearers were less attractive, and more than a quarter of them believed tattoo wearers were less intelligent than the rest of society. This judgment is irrational and unfair, but unless you plan to flash your Mensa membership card alongside your tattoos, you can expect over 25 percent of the people you encounter to assume you are dim.

Tattoos are not indelible and can be removed, most commonly with laser treatment. However, this requires a series of visits to the relevant clinic, may leave scarring, and is much more expensive than the original cost of the tattoo. If you yearn to look rebellious (as, rather sweetly, did a quarter of those with tattoos in the 2012 survey), why not opt for the temporary effect achieved by an ink transfer? Then you can imagine yourself as an edgy rule-breaker over the course of a weekend before reverting to societal norms on Monday morning. And nobody will question your level of intelligence. It can be asserted without contradiction that gentlemen do not have tattoos.

Piercings

Gentlemen are not pierced in any place. There was a fashion in late Renaissance courts for men to wear one earring, from which would hang something precious like a large baroque pearl. In 1577 the Anglican clergyman William Harrison published his *Description of England* in which he commented, "Some lusty courtiers and gentlemen of courage do wear either rings of gold, stones, or pearls in their ears." Like all fads, this one soon passed and men reverted to leaving their earlobes unpierced.

Piercing shares with tattoos both an ancient history and a popularity among primitive societies. The well-preserved mummy found on the Austro-Italian border in 1991 was not only heavily tattooed, he also had pierced ears. The world's oldest earrings, dating back to 2500 BC were found in a grave in the Sumerian city of Ur, once home to Abraham. And there are several Biblical references to earrings: during the Jewish exodus from Egypt, Aaron made a golden calf from melted earrings while Moses was otherwise preoccupied receiving the Ten Commandments on Mount Sinai.

It is not clear why people started to pierce their ears, although there seems to be consensus among historians that the practice had less to do with bodily adornment than with superstition: believing that demons could enter the body through ears, metal jewelry was placed in close proximity to ward them away. Later, sailors started to pierce their ears for various reasons: if they drowned, a gold earring would provide funds for a funeral; an earring was a symbol that the wearer had

If you have multiple piercings, you were most likely christened with a name like Jonathan, but now prefer to be known as Crusty, and participate in protests against global banking

traveled around the world; a pierced ear improved vision (although quite how is never explained).

Both male and female members of many tribes in Africa and Asia engage in ear piercing, although this does not customarily involve a tidy pair of pearl studs. Sometimes it can be a form of conspicuous consumption: the more piercings you have and the larger amount of costly metal, the greater your wealth. Certain tribes use piercing as a mark of transition from childhood to adolescence. Others don't just make a tiny hole but stretch the lobe to allow for the insertion of ear plugs.

If you are planning to move to a remote district of Borneo or perhaps the outer reaches of the Amazonian jungle, then these activities will be of interest and you will want to conform to societal norms that also include living in a hut and catching your own food. If, however, you have settled on Western norms, then having your ear pierced may not be such a good idea. While the practice has become more commonplace among men since the 1960s, it is still considered somewhat alternative and more frequently found among the young: there are few more regrettable sights than a middle-aged man sporting an earring. Rebellion is something best left to youth, especially when it takes the form of a pierced earlobe.

Earlobes are deemed to be erogenous zones, areas of our body especially sensitive to pleasure, and this helps to explain the popularity of earrings, since they draw the observer's attention.

Earlobes are deemed to be erogenous zones, areas of our body especially sensitive to pleasure, and this helps to explain the popularity of earrings

While women traditionally wear a pair of earrings, the preference among men has often been for just one. This is probably less a matter of aesthetics than a concern among insecure males that they should not be confused with the opposite sex. But among gentlemen, the preference remains for none at all. There are plenty of ways to ensure you receive attention without puncturing your ears.

Likewise the rest of your face. Since the advent of punk in the late 1970s, there has been a small sub-culture reveling in multiple piercings. So eyebrow, nostril and septum, lip, tongue, labret (the area between lower lip and chin) are all deemed ripe for a ring or stud, examples of which can be found among the more endangered tribes of Central Africa. If you do this to yourself, you were most likely christened with a name like Jonathan, but now prefer to be known as Crusty, live in a commune, follow a strict vegan diet, roll your own cigarettes, keep a mongrel dog attached to a piece of rope, and participate in countless protests against global banking. You are also most likely to have several other, more serious, grooming issues that ought to be dealt with posthaste.

It is, of course, perfectly possible to pierce any part of the human anatomy, and some people have done so. Unlike facial piercings, these marks are not immediately apparent, provided the person with them remains dressed. Only when clothes are removed do body piercings make an appearance, usually an unexpected one. As a rule, these adornments are associated with erogenous zones like the nipple, navel, and genitals, with the purpose of increasing sexual stimulation. A gentleman will not have such piercings, but should you encounter them in someone else, just make sure good hygiene has been followed. Given their location, piercings of this character need to be kept clean at all times.

Manscaping

There is a chance that you are unfamiliar with the word manscaping. If so, you are also likely to be unfamiliar with the practice of male depilation, otherwise known as the removal of body hair. This is a relatively modern phenomenon but one that appears to have widespread appeal, especially among younger members of society. A survey in August 2012 by Britain's *FHM* magazine found that 64 percent of its readership manscaped regularly and only 12 percent admitted to never doing so.

Various explanations are proffered to explain the emergence of depilation among men. Among the most likely is that for those who regularly frequent a gym and seek to develop their body shape, hair removal allows muscle form to be more clearly defined: notice how all body builders are hairless, at least whenever they are competing. In addition, pornographic actors—both male and female—tend to remove all or most of their body hair, again to give more prominence to the attributes that have brought them notice. It has been posited that with the advent of the internet and more widespread access to pornographic material, a greater number of people have judged body hairlessness as something to emulate. So, according to this theory, women started to remove all or most of their pubic hair because they had seen this trend among performers in adult films. Total hair removal, or what might be described as a carefully sculpted remnant, is thought to look tidier and, in many people's minds, to be cleaner.

Therefore, women have encouraged men to follow their example and remove most or all pubic hair for the same reasons.

Initially, manscaping was the preserve of that widely discussed but rarely sighted character, the metrosexual male—someone who was essentially urban in temperament and preoccupied with personal appearance. A frequently cited metrosexual role model is the previously mentioned David Beckham, whose bodily hairlessness (and fondness for tattoos) have been much copied.

So manscaping has moved beyond the world of porn and, as the *FHM* statistic demonstrates, gone mainstream. In April 2012, the *New York Times* reported that around 70 percent of one Manhattan salon's business involved male bikini waxing. How far you want to go with this is a matter of personal preference, as well as a reflection of your age and location: it is more likely manscaped bodies will be found among the young in large cities than among older country dwellers. Also variable are the means you use to remove your body hair. You can find electrical razors and trimmers for sale which allow the job to be done in the privacy of your own home. Alternatively, any urban center staking a claim to sophistication will have a salon capable of providing such a service to men using treatments already familiar to women, such as waxing. This requires wax to be applied to the body in strips, which are then pulled off, taking with them all the attached hair; the process is painful but effective. There

An entirely hairless man can look not unlike a freshly plucked chicken: so if you do plan to engage in manscaping, leave at least some evidence of your former hirsuteness

are creams available that do much the same thing with less discomfort, and there is even the possibility of permanent hair removal through electrolysis.

An entirely hairless man can look not unlike a freshly plucked chicken: scarcely the most enticing spectacle. So if you do plan to engage in manscaping, leave at least some evidence of your former hirsuteness. Think of the process as being similar to tidying up a garden; you want to keep the shrubbery neat rather than strip it bare. The only part of your anatomy that ought to be completely clear of hair is the back, which frequently sprouts growth from middle age onward. Remove every last follicle on your back, especially if you are planning to take off your clothes in public.

CHAPTER 16

Scents and Cosmetics

It's fascinating to see the various reasons advanced as to why humans wear perfume and have done so for thousands of years. Explanations fall into three broad categories, the first and most obvious being that scents hide other, less pleasant smells. There can be no doubt this was once a powerful argument in their favor but it holds less sway in our own age.

———◆———

Scent

It is proposed that far from masking our natural scent, perfumes heighten or fortify them as a way of sending out signals of attractiveness to other people. According to this theory, perfume acts as a magnet, although anyone who has ever stood next to somebody drenched in an unpleasantly powerful fragrance (there were a lot of them manufactured in the 1980s) will argue otherwise. It has also been suggested some perfumes contain chemicals that imitate human pheromones, a secreted or excreted chemical known to trigger a response in other humans and, in this instance, to encourage sexual attention. Whether this is true, or whether it is a hypothesis propounded by the perfume industry to encourage greater sales—as is evident in many advertising campaigns—remains open to question, not least because too little is known about the human reaction to pheromones.

A brief history

Whatever the rationale for its existence, scent has certainly been around for a long time. The word perfume derives from the Latin "per fumum," meaning "through smoke," which indicates just how old is this form of personal enhancement and also its original nature. For millennia before Christianity, fragrant woods and resins would be burnt during religious ceremonies as a form of homage to pagan deities; even today in the West, some Roman Catholic services incorporate a thurible, a metal vessel suspended on a chain in which incense is burned. And aromatic incense continues to be used in Hindu, Buddhist, and Taoist ceremonies.

At some point, it was decided that instead of burning fragrance we should wear it ourselves, using oils and resins derived from natural substances, which, when coming into contact with body heat, would exude their inherent perfume. This practice was widespread among Egyptians and then passed to the Greeks and Romans, who would anoint themselves with scent after bathing. It also became common practice to perfume a corpse before burial, although perhaps this was to counter the odor of decay, especially in warm climates. Many of the items we still associate with fragrance, like glass bottles and pots, were first produced in large quantities during the same period. Fragrances were taken from flowers like irises and roses, plants such as sandalwood and mint, and even spices like cinnamon. These were crushed and blended with pure oils before application.

Following the collapse of the Roman Empire in Western Europe from the 5th century onward, interest in perfume was superseded by

Perfume supposedly acts as a magnet for women, but anyone who has smelled somebody drenched in an unpleasantly powerful scent will argue otherwise

other concerns, most of them to do with basic survival. Further east, the Arabs developed the art of perfume making, refining the process of manufacture of fragrant oils and also perfumed waters. A key development was the discovery by the 11th-century Persian chemist and philosopher Ibn Sina, otherwise known as Avicenna, of how to extract essential oils from flowers and plants by means of steam distillation. The whole system of aromatherapy could not exist without his pioneering work in this field.

Some of Avicenna's voluminous writings on many subjects including medicine and health were translated into European languages. His process of perfume distillation was also adopted and formed the basis of all production until relatively recently. It was during the Renaissance period that perfume wearing once more became widespread, especially in Italy. When the Florentine Catherine de Medici married Henri II of France in 1533, she brought with her a personal perfumer, and his presence in Paris led to the city becoming a center of fragrance creation and manufacture, a status it has retained ever since. Likewise, the cultivation of flowers, essential for the extraction of their oils, became a major industry in the south of the country: the town of Grasse continues to be renowned in this regard.

Perfume wearing, among the affluent, was widespread for centuries, not least because it masked other, less savory smells. Napoleon Bonaparte, he who once wrote requesting his wife

Josephine not to wash as he would be home in three days, had two quarts of violet cologne delivered to him each week and, in addition, went through 60 bottles of double extract of jasmine monthly. Evidently there was little of our modern distinction between fragrances deemed suitable for men and those for women. This was a development of the 19th century when perfume production became more commercial in response to the rise of a middle-class market. Whereas, hitherto, perfume had been the preserve of wealthy elites, now it started to enjoy a broader appeal. Around the same time, advances in chemistry made it possible to re-create natural scents with man-made materials. The modern perfume industry was born.

The science of scent

Perfumery is both an art and a science, and creators of scents, known as "noses," need to combine the knowledge of a scientist with the creativity of an artist. A great deal has been written about perfumes, much of it as likely to induce queasiness as a cheap scent. However, if you want to learn more on the subject, finding informative texts is not difficult. But be warned: discussions about perfume are like those about wine, not least because both attract opinionated bores. In an effort to hold your attention, here is a synopsis of the various key facts you should know.

Like wine, perfume is composed of a sequence of "notes," which reveal themselves sequentially. Just as the wine in your mouth has an immediate taste, so too perfume has a top note, which is what you smell first. It rarely lasts more than a matter of minutes as the middle notes emerge, only to be supplanted in turn by the base notes—the core of the fragrance and the scent that you are going to smell in the hours ahead. Therefore, when you try a new fragrance in a department store or pharmacy, bear in mind that your immediate response to it will last no longer than do those top notes. You need to let the fragrance sit on your skin for some time before a full appreciation of it will be achieved.

Because there are now so many different fragrances on the market, they are usually divided into six groups, each with its own characteristics. Of these, floral is most popular with women but least with men because the latter associate it with the former: unlike Napoleon, today's man prefers not to douse himself in essence of jasmine. So-called Oriental scents are heavy and rich, with the evidence of spices and resins in their perfume. While they appeal to some men, they tend not to enjoy broad popularity. Citrus, on the other hand, which is tangy and refreshing with the zest of lime, lemon, and mandarin, does draw a broad constituency. So, too, do fragrances belonging to the fougère and chypre groups, since both have a mossy aroma. Fougère scents are inclined to be lighter, and chypre denser, but both are liked by men, as are green scents, which, as the name implies, tend to give the impression of natural freshness.

In case all that was insufficiently complicated, it must be explained that fragrances also come in different strengths, depending on the concentration of pure perfume they contain. Eau de parfum, or EDP, has between eight and 15 percent pure fragrance, while eau de toilette (EDT) has four to five percent. Aftershave and eau fraîche are lighter still, with anything between one and three percent pure perfume. Stronger scents are more expensive because the ingredients cost more. On the other hand, the higher the concentration of perfume, the longer lasting the fragrance. You get what you pay for.

Selecting a fragrance

Deciding what scent suits you best is a matter of trial and error. Of course, it's not obligatory: if you don't want to wear any fragrance at all, that's your prerogative. Some men think of themselves as incomplete without a fragrance, whereas plenty of others have never used one. But, having made the decision to wear some kind of scent, you should proceed the easiest way, which is to choose first which group you like best, be it chypre, citrus, or whatever. Then look at what's on offer within this field. Even so, there is such a bewildering variety of options available, it is not difficult to become overwhelmed. So another simplification is to stick with classics and let the sound, good taste of many other men help you: go for scents that have proven their appeal over previous decades. Manufacturers bring out new products every season, but few of them will stand the test of time. In fact, one of the hazards of selecting a new fragrance is precisely that it may be discontinued next year. A scent with a long history of success is more likely to remain in production and still be for sale long into the future.

As already advised, when you try a scent do bear in mind that it will smell different an hour or two after settling on the skin. So don't buy something just because you like how it smells immediately. Apply the fragrance on clean skin, ideally striaght after bathing or showering, and then let it settle. If you're still happy with the smell later in the day, then most likely this is the right fragrance.

There are certain key places where you should apply product, namely on the wrists, behind the ears, and on the neck; the skin is thin at these points and the fragrance will be more quickly absorbed. Don't overdo it: scent should complement your natural body aroma, not overwhelm it and every other smell within a range of several miles. Take into account that some people possess a more acute

*The higher the concentrations of perfume,
the longer lasting the fragrance*

sense of smell than others, and some are even allergic to modern scents, owing to the use of chemicals in their production. Be moderate in the application of any scent so that its presence is subtly apparent.

Finally, learn the value of loyalty, and make one scent distinctively your own. All of us possess a Proustian memory for smells, whether it is the aroma of particular meals we associate with childhood or the scent of someone we once loved. Wear the same fragrance for long enough and you will come to possess it in the minds of those who know you: every time they smell that scent, it will bring you to mind. This is the specific power of perfume, and it can be yours, too.

Men's cosmetics

In certain cultures and during certain periods men wore makeup, and sometimes just as much of it as women. The difference between the sexes did not extend to cosmetics: there are no stories of the ancient Egyptians dividing shades of eyeliner between boys and girls. Probably the last time men in any number wore makeup was the 18th century, although frequently this was to disguise or distract attention from skin problems such as pock marks caused by small pox. Come the 19th century, makeup for men fell out of favor as a more severe, and natural, look was preferred.

And that pretty much remains the case to the present day. Although there are periodic media stories about male cosmetics increasing in popularity, invariably these refer to skincare products like moisturizer rather than lipstick or mascara. Occasionally, someone in the public spotlight breaks ranks: ever since '70s shock rocker Alice Cooper, there have been musicians who decide to wear eyeliner in the hope of being noticed. This duly happens, and then they are ignored again. The fact is that for the past 200 years men have been discouraged from wearing makeup. As a rule, it is deemed effeminate and excessively vain, two traits the average man hopes he will never be accused of having.

Nevertheless, apparently more and more men are using cosmetics, albeit without ever declaring they do so publicly. The results of a survey released in January 2013 by online discount company HushHush.com showed that of more than 1,800 men polled, 11 percent admitted to wearing makeup, with over half that number doing so regularly, and one in five on a daily basis.

A little further investigation revealed precisely what these men were using, with 71 percent opting for concealer in order to hide skin blemishes or signs of tiredness under the eyes. Next in popularity came eyeliner and lipgloss, followed by mascara, although one suspects the number of men who wield a mascara brush with confidence is relatively small. The other popular item among men, as indicated by this and other similar surveys, is self-tan. More than a third of those in the HushHush.com poll said they used such a product, although some two-thirds of them preferred to do the job at home, with the rest prepared to be given a spray tan at a salon.

Aside from that rather startling statistic about eyeliner (49 per cent apparently), what these figures make clear is that when a man uses cosmetics, he intends them to enhance rather than alter his natural appearance. A tan is judged indicative of good health and considered attractive, whereas acne spots or bags under the eyes imply the reverse. Therefore one is added and the other hidden from view.

Concealers are certainly not to be eschewed. Applied with dexterity, they will do much to improve how you look on those days when you're suffering from sleep-deprivation or an unexpected outbreak of blemishes. They come in a variety of shades, so the first thing is to find that closest to your own skin tone and then employ with a deft hand. Just a little should do the trick: you're trying to conceal a problem, not bury it. Too much concealer will only draw attention to the blemish you intend to hide, so go easy for best results.

With regard to tans, although considered a sign of health, it is also now known that darkening your skin through exposure to the sun is liable to lead to cancer. Hence the popularity of fake tans, which mimic the real thing but without the inherent risks of overexposure to the sun.

If you decide to go down the route of fake tan, it is best to follow a couple of simple rules. First, set aside a bit of time and practice once or twice before your tan makes its public debut. Look around your supermarket or pharmacy and you will see plenty of possible products: choose one that is best for your skin type and is not too far removed from your present skin tone. The tan should be sheer, so that it is like a veil on your skin, and light so that your pores are not clogged. Remember that men's skin is thicker and coarser than that of women

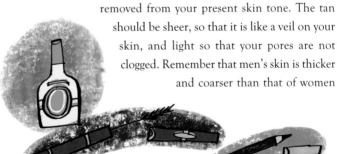

We have all seen people who look more tangerine than tan, due to excessive use of a faking product

and so anything other than the finest tan will leave a residue.

While coating your face with a layer of artificial tan does not require much skill, achieving good, even results on the rest of your body is much harder. You are quite likely to end up with parts of your anatomy featuring different shades. While your knees could be quite dark, for example, the area below them might still be pale or streaked like a piece of cheap bacon. Hair on your limbs makes fake tan harder to apply, as does our failure to have sufficiently long arms to reach the middle of our backs. A fake tan is best applied by a professional, who does this for a living and is therefore skilled at the task (and can be held responsible if the results are unsatisfactory). The sensible course of action is to visit a salon and have the job done properly.

Secondly, and just as important, whether on your face or anywhere else, choose a shade that looks natural. We have all seen people who look more tangerine than tan, due to excessive use of a faking product. Tempted though you may be to convey the impression of six months basking in the Bahamas, the probability is that everyone knows you were desk-bound in an office during the same period of time. The phrase "sun-kissed" is often used to describe a good tan. Interpret that to mean a friendly peck on the cheek, not a blazing smooch.

In other words, when it comes to fake tan, don't get carried away. Here, as in so many other areas of life, less is best. In fact, follow the same rule with regard to all aspects of makeup: operate with a sure but light hand.

CHAPTER 17

Diet and Exercise

Yet again, it was that indefatigable wordsmith St. Paul who first proposed the idea that our bodies are temples: he mentioned this in a letter to the Corinthians, so perhaps the Greek city's residents were particularly overweight. Whatever the case, his quote has resonated over the centuries, not least because many of us are aware that our own temples have become run down with age, or started to bulge at the external walls. Eventually we reach the point where a thorough program of restoration will be needed if the temple is to get back into decent condition.

———◆———

Diet

The ideal, of course, is ongoing maintenance rather than radical repair work. And one way to ensure your temple stays in good shape is to watch what you eat and drink. This becomes steadily more the case as we age. According to the American Dietetic Association, older men find it more difficult to keep down their weight due to a combination of decreasing lean body mass and increasing slothfulness. When young, we are full of energy and are therefore able to burn up a lot of calories. We engage with physical exercise and require an abundance of food to replenish our vitality. With the passage of time, however, our lives are inclined to become more static and our bodies less responsive to exertion. At the same time, our intake of food and drink remains the same or even increases, with the inevitable result that we put on weight.

So the first lesson to be learned is that, from around the age of 30, we should consider eating both less and with greater care if our waistband is not to grow. A 2010 study published in the *Journal of the American Medical Association* revealed that over 70 percent of men in the United States were either overweight or obese, with negative consequences for their general health and longevity prospects. A measure called the Body Mass Index (BMI) is commonly used to determine an individual's body fat based on weight and height. You can easily conduct this test on yourself, finding the relevant information on the internet. If your BMI is over 25, then you are deemed to be overweight, if over 30, obese.

Men are more likely to suffer from both these conditions than women for the same reason they are vulnerable to other health issues: failure to tackle the problem combined with an attitude peculiar to their gender, namely the irrational belief that ignoring an issue will lead to successful resolution. As a result, the numbers of overweight and obese men in Western society has grown, accompanied by a corresponding rise in certain conditions such as diabetes and heart disease.

Men diagnosed as suffering from one or both of these complaints are liable to find themselves advised on the importance of changing their diets. You can avoid reaching that point by watching what you eat and drink, and by keeping tabs on both the quality and quantity of your consumption. While some foods are better for us than others, nothing should be taken in excess. Moderation in all things must be your rule.

From the age of 30 we should consider eating less and with greater care if our waistband is not to grow

Food and drink are composed of a number of elements in different combinations: carbohydrates, proteins, fats, and vitamins and minerals. We need all of them to stay healthy but not equal measures of all. As the name indicates, carbohydrates contain carbon, hydrogen, and oxygen and are required by the body to produce energy. Derived from cereals, pulses, vegetables, and fruit, they include sugars and starch and are broken down in the body to form glucose. You need to be careful about your intake of carbohydrates because any glucose surplus to immediate requirements is stored in the liver and muscles as glycogen, which can potentially lead to diabetes.

Proteins have a similar composition to carbohydrates but with the addition of nitrogen. Found in meat, fish, dairy products, and eggs, protein can also be derived from some cereals and beans. It is necessary to us to enable growth, development, and repair of our bodies, as well as the production of enzymes, like those used for digestion, and hormones. Although often frowned upon, fats, also called lipids, are essential to your wellbeing. Found in meat, fish, and vegetable oils, fat is used to build nerves and the brain (40 percent of the latter is fat), insulate the body, produce hormones and cholesterol, and perform sundry other functions. Obtained from a variety of foodstuffs, vitamins and minerals are substances essential to ensure good health.

Eating healthily

And so to the specifics of your diet. First, a handful of rules you must follow without fail. Always eat a decent breakfast, and never skip it on the grounds of having insufficient time. Breakfast is the most important meal of the day and sets you up for what lies ahead. There is an old saying that we should breakfast like kings, lunch like princes, and dine like paupers. Even if you're anti-royalist, this makes excellent sense since it takes into account our body's metabolism and the process of burning calories through activity. In other words, consuming the largest amount of food at the start of the day and the least at its conclusion is the most beneficial approach. It is also essential that you eat three meals regularly, and around the same time each day, not just because you need the energy but also because setting up habitual patterns of behavior of this sort ensures you are less likely to snack. Your body responds well to consistency, and will not crave sustenance at odd hours if it is used to a daily intake of food on the same three occasions. Finally, try to eat something from every food group during each meal, because that way you are more likely to have a balanced diet.

That ideal balanced diet is most often known by the generic name of the Mediterranean Diet, based on the idea that it is consumed by peoples living around the periphery of the sea of the same name. Whether this is true or not, the main feature of the Mediterranean Diet is that it contains only moderate quantities of fat but a high intake of fruit and vegetables, whole grains, nuts, and seeds. It also features sufficient quantities of "good" fats known to be kind to the heart and arteries, such as olive and canola oil. Finally, while the Mediterranean Diet includes a reasonable amount of fish and poultry each week, it only allows for the consumption of red meat on a few occasions each month. Much of this food is rich in minerals and vitamins, low in calories, and high in fiber. In other words, it contains all the benefits of healthy eating, while leaving you feeling satisfied.

Not only will you keep down your weight by following a variant of the Mediterranean Diet, you will also reduce the possibility of suffering other illnesses such as heart disease and even some cancers.

Foods to avoid

By now, anyone with even a modicum of education will be aware that we ought to eat food as close to its raw condition as possible and shun refined foods like sugars. So you should steam vegetables rather than have them fried, and opt for fresh fruit over chocolate. While we need a certain amount of carbohydrates daily to provide us with sufficient energy for physical activity and cognitive function, we ought not to overdo it since carbohydrates also elevate blood-sugar levels, and not all of them are metabolized into energy. The Institute of Medicine in the United States recommends adults should receive 45-65 percent of dietary energy from carbohydrates, while the World Health Organization, in 2003, proposed a figure of 55–75 percent but recommended only ten percent of this come from sugars. On average it is proposed that carbohydrates make up 55 percent of your daily diet, fats 30 percent, and protein 15 percent.

The rules are not difficult, but nor are the reasons we fail to follow them: laziness, self-indulgence, a fondness for salt, fat, and sugar, and an erroneous belief that we are going to live forever. The last of these takes a blow first when we find it hard to run up even a short flight of steps without losing our breath, soon after which we are diagnosed with a serious coronary condition.

If this happens to you, then your doctor will most likely insist on a change in eating habits. Even without medical intervention, many men decide to alter their food consumption for the better. Opting for this season's fashionable diet is not recommended; many of them

Approach a lifestyle transformation slowly and make the changes at a leisurely pace

emphasize one food group at the expense of others, and also insist on too extreme an approach. Unless you have exceptional will power, you are liable to find shedding all your bad practices at the same time an enterprise impossible to sustain. Most likely you will fall back into the old ways: your health and waistline will not have improved, and nor your mood (or indeed your pocket since dieting plans always seem to require additional expenditure).

Approach a lifestyle transformation slowly and make the changes at a leisurely pace. Gradually shed the bad foods and adopt those known to be good for you. That way you will find it easier to keep going. While results might not appear as fast as you would wish, odds-on they will be permanent. It takes a while for body and mind alike to grow accustomed to a new regime, so don't rush things. And make sure to allow yourself an occasional reward: eating should be a pleasure, not a punishment.

What to drink

Obviously, all the previous information and advice also apply to your consumption of liquids. About 60 percent of our body is made up of water. Some of this is lost every day as we flush out toxins through bowel movements and urine, perspiration, and even breath. So it must be replenished if we are not to suffer from dehydration, which, in turn, leads to want of energy and lassitude. Some of this liquid we receive through food, but the greater part of it will be in the form of drinks. The

American Institute of Medicine has determined that an adequate intake of liquid for each day is three liters, which works out at about 13 cups.

The greater part of this should be taken as plain water. However, we also consume other liquids, most frequently tea, coffee, various sugared drinks, and alcohol. These can have positive effects, at least in the short term and in temperate quantities. Coffee, for example, acts as a stimulant, thanks to the presence of caffeine, and sometimes we require this in order to function, particularly when feeling tired. Similarly, a glass of wine with your meal can not only aid digestion but also lower the risk of heart disease, stroke, and diabetes.

As with food, what matters most is that you engage with all forms of drink with full awareness that moderation is best. One glass of wine may be good but that does not mean two glasses is better and three even more beneficial. Limit your intake of all liquids other than plain water, not least because, as a rule, they contain minimal nutrients. If you find yourself growing overly fond of, or dependent on, any of them, then it is best to wean yourself off entirely.

Exercise

No matter how good your diet, it will only be of limited benefit if not combined with some kind of exercise regime. The concept of exercise, as we understand it, is of relatively recent origin. Until the Industrial Revolution of the 19th century, the majority of men engaged in manual labor every day of their lives, mostly working in agriculture, in order to produce sufficient food for survival. Physical exertion was an inherent part of this process and therefore many of our forebears suffered from the consequences of too much, rather than too little exercise.

Our bodies evolved over millennia in the expectation that daily toil would be their lot. Now, however, the average male is no longer sweating in the fields but, instead, leads a sedentary existence. As a result, it is essential we put our bodies through their paces in some other way if they are not to undergo rapid degeneration through lack of use. Hence the importance of exercise.

Just as most of us don't relish the idea of plowing or picking root vegetables, so we are disinclined to approach exercise with delight. Mankind is inherently indolent, and it is important to understand and accept this fact. Exercise requires effort, both physical and mental, and the second of these is just as critical as the first. Other than full-time sportsmen, few of us regard physical activity with relish. On the other hand, once we have embarked on even a short bout of exercise, we are likely to feel better. Scientific research has shown that exertion increases levels of endorphins and serotonin in the brain, both of which play a part in establishing our sense of well-being. Furthermore, rises in core body temperature and increased blood flow to the brain, both of which occur during exercise, trigger mood improvement. Finally, although less easy to monitor, it is widely accepted that regular exercise leads to better self-image and greater confidence, which, in turn, is advantageous to our mental health. There is also research indicating that exercise promotes better sleep: all of us know that when we are physically tired, we fall asleep quicker and remain asleep longer than on those occasions when we haven't stirred from the sofa all day. In other words, while we may be temperamentally reluctant to embark on exercise, once this barrier is overcome we immediately experience the advantages, not least psychological.

Although we are usually aware of the importance of exercise and know we will look and feel better for engaging in physical activity,

> *Exercise requires effort, both physical and mental, and the second of these is just as critical as the first*

nevertheless we remain reluctant to do so. The problem is that, in our culture, exercise has come to be represented as extreme activity and, accordingly, appears unappealing, especially at the onset. According to British government statistics, only 37 percent of men take sufficient exercise to derive any benefit from it, with consequences for the health of the nation. Surely at least part of the explanation for this low number is the way in which exercise is usually characterized as some kind of demanding challenge that will leave us feeling debilitated.

Keep it simple

On the contrary, it is perfectly possible to reach the required quota of exercise without too much effort. Adult males should engage in a minimum of 30 minutes moderate-to-reasonably-intense physical activity at least five days a week. This means you must feel at least some sense of exertion and increased body warmth, but not that you are draped over a gym weight machine gasping for breath and dripping sweat. A brisk walk will do the trick, as will climbing stairs (as opposed to taking the elevator) or cycling (as opposed to taking the bus). Even better, the 30 minutes do not need to follow each other consecutively: as long as you spend at least that much time each day in exercise, even if broken into smaller units of five or ten minutes, then you will enjoy all the rewards. If you are seriously out of shape, diagnosed as obese, or deemed at risk from conditions such as diabetes, then the amount of time required to be spent exercising is likely to increase, rising to a minimum of one hour each day. Yet again this is proof of the advantages of keeping yourself in good condition.

As we grow older it becomes still more critical that exercise has a daily place in our lives. Remaining in good physical condition renders us better able to look after ourselves and not be dependent on others. It is also clear that elderly people who are physically healthy are more likely to be mentally in good shape, too. If you want to live long and well, sloth is not to be considered.

How to enjoy exercising

Should you plan to embark on an exercise regime more strenuous than a daily walk, then bear in mind the following key points.

* Choose an activity that you are most likely to enjoy. There's no point torturing yourself with long-distance marathons if you hate running even to catch a train. Some forms of exercise are understandably more popular than others, like cycling or swimming. Not only do these improve your state of health but they do so in a way that is relatively undemanding.

* Pace yourself. If you haven't undertaken any exercise for a long time, then start slowly. Set yourself achievable goals and gradually build up to them: once they're reached, you can always give yourself a greater challenge. Don't be unrealistic about what's possible; it takes time to get fit and, especially if you are past your twenties, your body will no longer be able to do as much as once might have been the case.

✱ Wear appropriate clothing. An obvious tip you might think, but an astonishing number of people don't understand that the clothes they wear every day to work are not suited for exercise. In particular, invest in a pair of decent sports shoes, which will give your feet the support they need when engaging in physical activity. Inappropriate footwear can put unnecessary strain on other parts of your body, not least your knees and back, with the threat of consequent injury.

✱ Consider joining a group or club, or even starting one. Many of us, when we decide to get into shape, think of the enterprise as a solitary activity. On the contrary, there are plenty of exercise regimes that depend on a number of participants: you could join a local soccer group, for example. One of the advantages to doing something like this is that the other members act as a spur to ensuring you remain committed. It's easy to put off exercise when this involves a solitary run in the winter rain but harder when the rest of the team is waiting for you to turn up.

Exercise becomes less burdensome and more fun when it is participatory, and when there's a social element to the experience. For the same reason, if you take up swimming or cycling or even walking, look for local groups engaging in the activity. Most public swimming pools, for example, have classes for a number of people at a time. The hardship of exercise won't seem so bad when the experience is shared with other people.

You could, of course, opt for working out in a gym. Our ancestors would surely be first baffled and then amused by establishments where the clientele pay money to engage in physical toil. And, indeed, it remains somewhat extraordinary that, with so many forms of exercise available free, the

Research indicates that exercise promotes a better night's sleep

most obvious being a daily walk, large numbers of people decide instead to be charged for the same thing. Obviously gyms have equipment and facilities that you most likely will not have at home, whether weight machines or a swimming pool. Many of these devices allow you to build up and improve the musculature of certain parts of your body, and there are instructors to supervize you while doing so. This is their unique selling point and one that enjoys widespread popularity. So if you do wish to bulk up your arms or chest or legs or all of them and more besides, then a gym is to be recommended.

There is another advantage to gyms, even if not one intended by their owners: having spent money on membership fees, you are more likely to turn up and use the facilities than would be the case if you were embarking on a free regime. That, at least, is the theory. Ten years ago, however, a survey in Britain discovered the drop-out rate for gyms was 80 percent. In other words, four out of five people, having paid membership fees—which are usually quite substantial— then opted not to take advantage of the facilities on which they had spent money. If ever there was evidence of our reluctance to engage with exercise, it comes from this statistic. Also apparent is the fact that spending money cannot automatically be equated with improving your health or physique: if this were the case, we could all choose to be poor but fit. We would then be just like the majority of our ancestors, except they had no choice in the matter. Such are the vagaries of human nature.

Index